Lightship Baskets
of Nantucket

Text and Photography by
Martha Lawrence

Revised & Expanded 2nd Edition

Dedication

To my sons, Douglass and Matthew, whose courage, goodness and ready wit bring me incredible joy and pride.

Revised: 2000
Copyright © 1990 & 2000 by Martha R. Lawrence
Library of Congress Catalog Card Number: 99-68524

ISBN: 0-7643-0891-2
Printed in China
1 2 3 4

Published by Schiffer Publishing Ltd.
4880 Lower Valley Road
Atglen, PA 19310
Phone: (610) 593-1777; Fax: (610) 593-2002
E-mail: Schifferbk@aol.com
Please visit our website catalog at
www.schifferbooks.com

This book may be purchased from the publisher.
Include $3.95 for shipping. Please try your bookstore first.
We are interested in hearing from authors
with book ideas on related subjects.
You may write for a free printed catalog.

In Europe, Schiffer books are distributed by
Bushwood Books
6 Marksbury Avenue
Kew Gardens
Surrey TW9 4JF England
Phone: 44 (0)208-392-8585; Fax: 44 (0)208-392-9876
E-mail: Bushwd@aol.com

Preface

Long before I ever owned or imagined constructing a Nantucket Lightship Basket, I appreciated their symmetry and simple grace. That these baskets were uniquely and inextricably linked to a place of great influence in my life made them even more appealing.

As I began to learn the process of construction, I became more impressed with the skill of those who have produced the fine baskets of yesterday and today and I came to appreciate the baskets on a different level.

The opportunity to photograph a variety of old and new Nantucket Lightship Baskets for this volume has served to further heighten my appreciation of their texture, form, and color and my admiration for their makers. I am proud to be a small part of this old and lovely craft and happy to share the story of these baskets.

Acknowledgements

For their assistance with the research and historical photographs in this volume, I would like to thank Jacqueline Harring, Gail Michael, Betsy Cotting, and Peter MacGlashan of the Nantucket Historical Association and also Ruth Thibideau and Kathy Flynn of the Peabody Museum of Salem. For their encouragement and support I am grateful to Sherry Mattison, Charles and Olive Welton, Lynn Petrasch, Carolie Frazer, Daphne Prout, Barbara Leith, Pattie Kaczynski and Dianne Reich.

Special thanks are due Paul and Diane Madden for allowing me to photograph their wonderful collection of Nantucket Lightship Baskets, and for their encouragement and suggestions.

No author could have a more supportive editor than Nancy Schiffer. Thank you. The photographs of the actual construction process were taken by Schiffer editor Tim Scott, whose patience and sense of humor during the process were much appreciated.

And finally, thanks to Sue Brooks, who many years ago asked,"Do you want to come over and make a lightship basket?", to Reggie Reed, who patiently explained the mysteries of finishing the woven basket; to Alan Reed for both his instruction and my first oval mold; to Bob and Karen Marks for their generous help and guidance; and to Tom LeFevre for his many years of beautiful woodworking and friendship.

Contents

Introduction

Nantucket, a mere sand bar thirty miles off Cape Cod, has experienced renown perhaps surprising in view of its size and location. In the eighteenth and nineteenth centuries, it was recognized throughout the globe for its dominance in the whaling trade. The profits of this and ancillary industries built a prosperous, bustling community.

The mid-nineteenth century decline of whaling and coincidental economic misfortunes brought hard times to the island. Population declined and little new construction took place. Although unintentional, this lack of progress preserved eighteenth and early nineteenth century buildings, sparing them from alteration or replacement. Today, the streets of Nantucket are a museum of beautifully designed and preserved homes.

By the late nineteenth century, the island's appeal was becoming apparent to travellers, and Nantucket welcomed the first waves of tourism that would become to the island's economy what whaling had been a century before.

Today, Nantucket is bustling once more. Attracted by the magnificent ocean, rolling moors, and historic town are not only short-term visitors but also summer residents from whose rambling old houses tumble barefoot children anxious to be reunited each year with grandparents, cousins, and the island's natural attractions.

Nantucketers, both "legitimate" and "adopted", take pride in their island and its history. Included in this history is the story of the Nantucket Lightship Basket, conceived and refined by pragmatic Nantucketers and fashioned for over a century by men determined to preserve both the craft and its high quality. Today it is appreciated and sustained by a growing year-round and summer population for whom the basket has become a tangible reminder of their island's legacy and a treasured heirloom to pass on to future generations.

As whaling ships once spread Nantucket's influence to the far corners of the world, the Nantucket Lightship Basket has likewise become an ambassador for the island, acquainting those far from its shores with Nantucket's heritage and high standards.

Chapter 1
Basket Beginnings

The Nantucket Lightship Basket evolved into a distinct entity, distinguishable from all other baskets, over many decades. Many influences contributed to its eventual design, such as the simple weaving pattern of native Indian basketry. However, it was Nantucket's chief eighteenth-century industry, whaling, and the related trade of coopering that influenced the basket's framework and reliance on woodworking skills. As the basket developed, the geographical isolation of Nantucket, an island thirty miles off the coast of Massachusetts, insured its metamorphosis into the unique basket we know today.

Eighteenth-century Nantucketers had need for a wide range of baskets-heavy agricultural baskets, sturdy storage baskets, and more delicate house baskets. The latter were used for sewing, wool storage, knitting, berry gathering, and countless other pursuits. There was a basket for every task.

Islanders were familiar with the baskets of local Algonkian Indians. (The designation "Algonkian" refers to a common language grouping shared by Nantucket Indians and other New England tribes.) In fact, records show Algonkian Indians selling baskets to Starbuck's "store" as early as 1686.[1] Nantuck-

These nineteenth-century baskets typify the durable, tightly woven Nantucket Lightship Basket. *Collection of the Welton family.*

The balance and symmetry found in Nantucket's architecture is also inherent in the Nantucket Lightship Basket.

eters also were importing both Indian and European baskets from the mainland. In 1802 Mashpee Indians from Cape Cod are recorded as frequently traveling to and selling baskets on Nantucket.[2] The necessity of importing baskets resulted from not only the demand but also from the absence of a full-time basket maker on the island. As Charles and Mary Grace Carpenter conclude in their meticulously researched *The Decorative Arts and Crafts of Nantucket,* "There was no one called a basket maker in either the land court or probate records of Nantucket in the seventeenth and eighteenth centuries."[3]

Algonkian baskets of this period were woven with rush, bark, cornhusks, and other fibers. The wooden splint basket that influenced the Nantucket Lightship Basket was a later development. It was constructed with thin splints of wood obtained by laboriously beating logs to separate the growth rings. There is no mention of Indian splint basketry prior to 1712, and some researchers suspect that it began among the Delaware, either invented by them or introduced to them by German and Swedish settlers. The use of woodsplints is believed to have then spread in waves toward the Northeast, where it was adopted by the Algonkians.[4]

Eighteenth-century Nantucketers already familiar with Algonkian splint basketry through trade began to duplicate these baskets and adapt them to their own requirements. Indian splint baskets, with their woven checker-board bottoms, were suited primarily to light tasks. Strengthening the basket bottoms for heavy farm chores was one of the first requirements, and rounded, "spider web" bottoms were woven to replace the weaker grid bottoms. Before long, woven bottoms were omitted altogether and replaced with sturdy planks of wood. This adaptation links the developing basket to the wooden casks of the cooperage trade, flourishing in Nantucket in the eighteenth and first half of the nineteenth centuries.

In this period the economy of Nantucket was linked inextricably to the whaling industry. From

These early splint baskets have bottoms woven in a checker-board pattern. *Collection of the Nantucket Historical Association.*

16

An early example of what would come to be called a Nantucket Lightship Basket. Rather than one slotted piece of wood serving as a base, this 8 1/2" basket has two pieces of wood nailed together that hold the staves between them. *Collection of the Nantucket Historical Association.*

Nantucket ships set forth to the far reaches of the Pacific in search of the whales whose oil lit lamps around the world. In turn a great demand was created for wooden casks in which to store the precious oil aboard ship and later ashore. Not surprisingly, a good proportion of Nantucketers engaged in the coopering trade in response to this demand. A tabulation compiled by the Carpenters indicating the occupations of Nantucketers between 1701 and 1776 lists 189 men as coopers, a group in size second only to mariners, who numbered 304.[5]

Joseph E.C. Farnham, reminiscing on his Nantucket boyhood, describes the products of cooper David Folger. "In those cooper shops were made the casks, splendidly fashioned...so carefully made, with flagging between the staves to make them positively tight, securely bound with heavy iron hoops."[6] In addition to these casks, coopers were responsible for the many wooden buckets and tubs so well constructed that many rendered years of service for their owners and survive today.

As it has for over 150 years, the Pacific National Bank stands guardian at the head of cobble-stoned Main Street overlooking the harbor. Nantucket-bound whaling ships brought home their wealth to this harbor.

Hundreds of casks of whale oil unloaded in 1870 on Merrill's Wharf,
New Bedford, Massachusetts, testify to the importance of coopers to
the whaling trade. *Collection of the Peabody Museum of Salem.*

Coopers were important not only on shore as adjuncts to the whaling industry but also aboard ship. Each whaling vessel carried its own cooper. Before being placed on the ship, many casks were taken down or "shooked" as a space-saving measure. These shooked casks were later reassembled by the ship' s cooper as one of his duties.

Although statistics reveal a large number of men whose primary occupation was coopering, other Nantucketers knew enough of the trade to employ it for their own needs or to fill the demand for products unmet by "professional" coopers. In his 1722 account of the "Peculiar Customs at Nantucket," Hector St. John Crèvecoeur comments on the universality of the coopering craft on the island.

Idleness is the most heinous sin that can be committed in Nantucket... They are never idle... They always have a piece of cedar in their hands, and while they are talking, they will...employ themselves in converting it into something useful, either in making bungs or spoyls for their oil casks, or other useful articles. I must confess, that I have never seen more ingenuity in the use of the knife... They have shewed me a variety of little bowls and other implements, executed cooperwise, with the greatest neatness and elegance... They are all brought up to the trade of coopers, be their future intentions or fortunes what they may; therefore almost every man in this island has always two knives in his pocket... They are as difficult to please, and as extravagant in the choice and price of their knives, as any young buck in Boston would be about his hat, buckles, or coat.[7]

Many of Nantucket's gracious homes were built with
the profits of the whaling industry.

It was these many "occasional" as well as "full-
time" coopers whose skill contributed to the development of the Nantucket Lightship Basket. The
basic construction of a wooden cask is so similar to
the skeleton of a lightship basket that their relation-
ship is undeniable. Like the basket the cask grows
from a board bottom, its body is comprised of up-
right wooden staves and large hoops hold it together.
Even the closeness of staves and tightness of weaving, hallmarks of a well-made lightship basket, are
akin to the tight, flagged construction of the casks
and buckets designed by coopers to hold liquids.

This sturdy wooden-staved twelve-inch basket reveals
its origins in Nantucket's coopering tradition. *Collection of the Welton family.*

The wooden bottoms used in early baskets were not the intricately turned pieces used later in the nineteenth century. Rather than the one solid piece of wood turned on a lathe and slotted around the edge, early basket bottoms often were two round pieces of wood nailed together to hold the staves between them. Thrifty Nantucketers did not visit the local hardwood supplier to purchase bottom wood, but used whatever scrap lumber was available to build the basket. Basket bottoms sometimes sported the printing of a recycled commercial box or the paint of a discarded piece of lumber. By the time baskets were being made aboard the *New South Shoals* lightship, the sycamore wood of plug tobacco boxes reportedly was favored for bottoms. Whether for their tobacco or their sycamore box, "B.L." and "Lorillard's" were reportedly the most popular brands.[8] Pine was used for bottoms in very early baskets before the use of hardwoods such as maple, cherry, and mahogany became the norm.

As Nantucket basket makers became more adept at their craft, there arose a desire for more precisely sized and formed baskets. A basket whose exact capacity was established could also be used as a measure of goods. Furthermore, differently sized baskets of uniform shape could be nested inside one another for both aesthetic pleasure and more practical economy of space in the small homes of nineteenth-century Nantucket. To achieve this uniformity in size and form, basket makers began weaving the

These seven baskets by Captain James Wyer, ranging in size from 5 1/2" to 12 3/8", well demonstrated the space-saving attributes of nesting. *Collection of the Nantucket Historical Association.*

The blue bottom of this graceful, rattan-staved basket probably was painted after construction so that its owner could readily identify it while berrying or attending a church supper. *Collection of the Nantucket Historical Association.*

Each of these baskets was woven on an individual, hand-made wooden mold. *Collection of the Welton family.*

baskets over "blocks" now more commonly referred to as molds. These often were sections of old broken spars and masts.

The use of molds made the actual shaping of the basket easier, because the mold dictated the shape of the basket. (When weaving without a mold, the basket maker shapes the basket by the tension on the weaver.) However, although the actual basket shaping was easier, designing and executing the molds themselves required ingenuity, skill, and an eye for proportion. The construction of molds no doubt was a challenge to the creativity of the makers and a chance to further display their skills at wood-working by carving beautifully graduated nests of molds similar to the "elegant little bowls" described by Crèvecoeur.

Over the years this use of wooden bottoms and molds on which to weave the baskets became common to island baskets and now are considered two of the distinguishing characteristics of the Nantucket Lightship Basket. As mentioned, both the staves and weavers (horizontal components) of early transitional baskets were thin wooden splints obtained by the same time-consuming process employed by the Indians. In an effort to increasingly strengthen the basket and speed up the material preparation, basket makers once more borrowed from the cooperage and began to split staves with drawknives and shaving horses similar to the one being used by Mitchell Ray and shown on page 57.

Also, the wooden splints used as weavers were being replaced with rattan, a long, climbing vine whose bark is known to us as cane. Rattan found its way to Nantucket from its home in the Pacific in the holds of whaling vessels. Rattan's advantages became readily apparent to the Nantucketers. The vine could be split into strips both longer and more flexible than wooden splints, it had a naturally glossy finish, and most importantly it was available and abundant. Before committing themselves entirely to rattan, however, some basket makers wove a few experimental rows with cane and finished the basket with wooden splints. At the beginning of a basket, the weaver has to travel in small circles in a relatively tight space. Perhaps the makers of these "transitional" baskets were experimenting with the rattan and its adaptability for concise work. At any rate, baskets soon were woven exclusively with rattan and began to be called "rattan baskets." As with the use of molds and wooden bottoms, the rattan weaver became an essential component of a Nantucket Lightship Basket.

The staves of this 9 1/2" basket are roughly cut slab-rattan. The rim and ear are of wood. *Private collection.*

A "transition" basket. The first eight rows of this gaily painted 6 1/4" basket are woven with rattan. The remainder of the basket is woven with wood splints. Rattan is used again to lash the rim. The owner's initials, "WSC," are carved in the handle. *Collection of Paul and Diane Madden.*

Some Nantucket basket makers also experimented with rattan for staves. Joseph Farnham's account of basket making in his father's shop in the early 1850s refers to rattan staves or "ribs." "Those ribs were fashioned from large splint cane, carrying the round edge on the outer side, with the flat surface on the inner."[9] Rattan also was used for staves when an extremely delicate-looking basket was the goal. However, except for the years 1850 to 1870, when cane staves also were utilized, the staves of choice remained the hardwoods-oak, ash, hickory.

Although it is impossible to state with certainty the period by which the "rattan basket" had developed into an identifiable entity, it is estimated by most students of the subject to have been about the 1820s or 1830s. This basket, only later to be known as a Nantucket Lightship Basket, was characterized by a wooden bottom, rattan weavers, and its construction on a wooden mold. Similar techniques were found in baskets of other areas: Shaker baskets were woven on molds, and many New Hampshire farm baskets were built from sturdy wooden bottoms. However, only Nantucket's rattan baskets combined the elements of wooden bottoms, rattan weavers, and mold construction exclusively. Nantucket's geographical isolation no doubt contributed to the climate in which these baskets could slowly develop into a unique form influenced by Indian crafts, whaling exploration, and the ingenuity and skill of the coopering Nantucketers.

The rattan basket certainly was an identifiable form by the early 1850s, when Farnham wrote of its construction in his father's shop. The men described shared a disdain for idleness with the Nantucketers mentioned by Crèvecoeur 125 years earlier. They were busily working "for pleasure rather than for profit." His description of their activity is not only a detailed but also an intimate vision of the life of the time.

That little iron cylinder stove, radiating its comforting heat, was a magnet around which a number of men used to sit and indulge in that occupation. Of them I well recall the genial Capt. George F. Joy and the ever-pleasant and agreeable Mr. Charles G. Coggeshall. Each of them worked while "pulling" upon one of the then so popular...clay pipes, evidently fully enjoying the smoke derived therefrom. I delighted to sit and listen to their entertaining conversa-

In this more refined, rattan-staved nine-inch basket, the rim also is rattan. *Private collection.*

A rattan-staved basket believed to date from the period described by Joseph Farnham. Used for gathering beach plums, it remains a working part of this summer household. *Private collection.*

A nine-inch "rattan-basket" at home in an atmosphere of nautical memorabilia. *Private collection.*

tion and story-telling. A boy, then ten to twelve years of age, I soon learned...the art of making those baskets-for art it really was...We called them rattan baskets. They were made in varying sizes from very small up to about the capacity of a peck. In slight graduation...those baskets were placed one within the other in so-called "nests". As so arranged they made a most inviting appearance. "Work baskets" for the ladies were made quite large...with a woven cover, hinged at the side, and they were certainly very neat and pretty... Those men, some retired from service at sea on a whale-ship, others temporarily idle, most profitably employed their spare hours in the manner narrated.[10]

The rattan basket was a fixture in the lives of many Nantucketers by the 1850s. The next period of its development-the lightship period-gave the rattan basket the name by which we know it today.

Footnotes

[1] Charles H. Jr. and Mary Grace Carpenter, *The Decorative Art and Crafts of Nantucket*(New York: Dodd, Mead and Co., 1987), p.183.
[2] Katherine and Edgar Seeler, *Nantucket Lightship Baskets*(Nantucket: The Deermouse Press, 1972), p. 3.
[3] Carpenter, *Decorative Arts*, p. 185.
[4] Ann McMullen, *Artifacts*, Fall 1982, p. 1.
[5] Carpenter, *Decorative Arts*, p. 225.
[6] Joseph E.C. Farnham, *Brief Historical Data and Memories of My Boyhood Days in Nantucket* (Providence: Snow and Farnham Co., 1923)p. 172.
[7] J. Hector St. John Crèvecoeur, *Letters from an American Farmer*(New York: Fox, Duffield and Co., 1904) pp. 204-205.
[8] Harry B. Turner, "The South Shoals Station and the Vessels That Have Guarded It From 1854-1931," *The Inquirer and Mirror*, May 16, 1931.
[9] Farnham, *Boyhood Days in Nantucket*, p. 170.
[10] Ibid., pp. 169-170.

A cool breeze sends clouds scudding past the steeple of
Nantucket's Congregational Church.

This feline remains unimpressed by the history around her.

The "Nantucket" station was the most exposed position of any U.S. lightship. The danger of the location was confirmed six months later when a northeast gale snapped the heavy anchor chain and blew the *Number 11* fifty miles to be grounded on Montauk Point, New York. Only the skill of former whaling master Captain Samuel Bunker and his crew saved the ship from being smashed on the very shoals she was guarding. Despite this exhibition of seamanship, Mrs. Bunker, who had never favored her husband's new command, requested that he retire from the lightship service after this experience.

The Nantucket shoals were left unmarked once more until a replacement vessel was built. A larger, sturdier ship was built of oak in the Kittery, Maine, navy yard. She was built with two hulls, to protect the ship in collisions. The space between these was filled with salt. This "sweetener" successfully hardened the wood to the extent that it reportedly "defied the carpenter's brace and bit."[5]

Nantucket's South Tower. It was from this height that a watchman, routinely scanning the horizon at daybreak for vessels in distress, discovered that the *Number 11* had broken adrift of her mooring and was missing.

Portrait of Captain Samuel Bunker, commander of the ill-fated *Number 11*, first lightship to serve on the South Shoal station. *Collection of the Nantucket Historical Association.*

28

Photographed by Nathaniel L. Stebbins on a calm day, the *New South Shoal* rides serenely at anchor. The beacon lights are not visible as they were lowered into the deck houses each morning. *Collection of the Peabody Museum of Salem.*

This replacement vessel, named *Number 1 Nantucket, New South Shoal,* was a 103-foot schooner. Her two seventy-one-foot masts each carried a beacon consisting of eight oil lamps. Built around the base of each mast was a small house into which the lamps were lowered to be cleaned and filled. The housing was necessary to prevent the lamps from being damaged or even washed away by the heavy seas so common to the area. In addition to the beacons, a large bell also warned ships of her location. Behind each mast was a shorter mast for sails, the only power. The *New South Shoal* was built for strength and endurance rather than beauty and, like many lightships, her appearance was somewhat clumsy.

She was placed in service in January 1856.

Serving aboard the new ship were Captain Allen H. Gifford and a ten-man crew, all Nantucketers. Both the dangerous location and the harsh New England weather made life extremely hazardous for the men aboard. The wild pitch and roll of the moored lightship, so different from the smoother motion of a vessel underway, was at best uncomfortable. Bunks were tilted inward to prevent the crew from being tossed from them as the ship plunged and lurched. Closeness of the quarters was intensified by the portholes, always closed due to the rolling of the ship. For the same reason, pots and kettles had to be lashed to the stove. Despite this precaution it was not uncommon for a side of pork to fly from the stove and land in a nearby bunk!

This routine discomfort paled, however, in comparison to life during a storm. As the wind and seas raged, the ship would saw and rasp at the chains that moored her. First riding the crest of a wave and then plunging into its trough, the lightship would roll and ship water on one side of the deck, and then on the other. One captain commented that the ship "washed her own decks." A crewman serving aboard a later, twentieth-century lightship in the same location described the height of the waves. "It was frightening to look out the porthole on the bridge and see the crest of the wave still above you."[6]

This later vessel, *Number 106*, rides out a 1926 winter gale, confirming reports of waves higher than the bridge of the ship. *Collection of Nantucket Historical Association.*

In the midst of this turmoil, the crew would attend to their duties, groping their way along the deck under the gyrating beacon lamps, doused by waves and tossed by the pitching of the ship. Yet regardless of the conditions, lightships could not leave their stations unless relieved by another ship. An 1829 directive to lightship keepers ordered them "not to slip or cut the cable..in any event, and if the vessel should be likely to founder, to abandon her with the crew."[7]

Lightships did, however, often leave their stations. The *New South Shoal* broke adrift twenty-three times in her thirty-six years of service, leaving over twenty huge mushroom anchors on the ocean floor. The most notable experience occurred in October 1878 in a severe northeast gale. After parting her mooring chain, the *New South Shoal* was driven 80 miles off station, completing her unscheduled journey just off Bermuda. The winds were favorable enough so that the damaged ship was able to return under sail, but often in such circumstances the lightship had to be towed back to her station.

Cold weather added to the general discomfort. In winter the sea spray froze to the ship, shrouding her in several feet of ice. The crew became accustomed to the eerie sound of wind shrieking through ice-encrusted rigging.

Danger from the shifting shoals, unpredictable currents, and inclement weather was compounded by the threat of the very marine traffic the ship was there to warn. To avoid the shoals, passing vessels headed straight for the lightship. European-bound ships aimed for the lightship to get an accurate line of departure. Similarly, incoming navigators welcomed the lights of the *New South Shoal* not only as a haven from the dangerous shoals but also for the knowledge that they were then but 200 miles east of New York.

The ever-present danger of a collision with a ship setting its course for the lightship was increased by the heavy fog that blanketed the area forty percent of the year. Although the *New South Shoal* never was involved in a collision, a later lightship (*Number 117*) was sliced in half by the New York-bound liner *Olympic*, killing seven of the crew in 1934.

More overwhelming perhaps for the captain and crew than the danger of high seas or of ships bearing down on them in heavy fogs was the loneliness of life aboard the lightship. Twice between spring and fall each crew member would go ashore for two months, serving a total of eight months aboard ship. Disputes in such confinement became magnified and required Solomonic wisdom on the part of the captain responsible for arbitration. In a few instances feelings ran so deeply that families on Nantucket were not on speaking terms due to a dispute on the lightship.[8]

Below a painting of a storm-tossed vessel rests a model of an early lightship. Included in the details is the beacon light built around the mast and the opened deck house into which the beacon was lowered in the daylight hours. *Collection of Paul and Diane Madden.*

Aerial view of decommissioned lightship *Number 112* temporarily anchored off Nantucket Harbor gives a sense of the vastness of the ocean compared to the size of ship.

The narrow strip of beach at left is the Haulover, the route taken into Nantucket Harbor by James Wood and friends. The considerable length of this row can be better realized by a glance at the navigational chart on page 26.

The records of the lightship service, however, generally emphasize the cooperation of the men aboard. One keeper credits his men's attitude in a storm: "Everybody did his full share of work cheerfully...They did what they could to keep things fast and shelter themselves as best they could during the worst of gale."[9]

In addition, the monotony of shipboard life did have its lighter moments. On September 9, 1860, Captain Obed Coffin hailed a passing schooner to learn the results of the presidential election. "Abe Lincoln, of Illinois!" was the answer that came floating back to the news-starved crew.[10]

That any diversion was a welcome break for the crew was amply demonstrated by James H. Wood's "row for butter." As shipboard provisions were running low, Captain Benjamin Morris ordered Mr.

Wood and five men to row to Nantucket, an arduous twenty-five mile row. Shortly after setting off, thick fog closed in and Captain Morris signaled the men to return. Perhaps the men did not hear the signal or more likely were so anxious for some time ashore that they ignored it. Despite the heavy fog and the long, hard row, they remained on their course for Nantucket. It was hours before they first sighted land. After crossing the Haulover, a narrow beach, they reached the head of Nantucket harbor, where they spent the night. The following morning they continued their row down harbor to town. When asked by startled townsfolk whether the lightship had burned or sunk. Wood calmly replied, "We just ran out of butter, so thought we had better come ashore and get some."[11]

Of course, such adventures were limited to good weather. Isolation for the lightship crew was more the norm. A marvelous article that emphasizes the loneliness of life aboard the lightship was written for *Century Magazine* by Gustave Kobbe, who visited the *New South Shoal* in 1891. Then moored a few miles further southeast of her first station, the lightship was totally dependent on the tender *Verbena* for provisions, news, and mail. However, once winter descended, weather conditions prevented the *Verbena* from servicing the lightship. On calm days she would venture far enough to spot the blur of the lightship on the horizon and report her safely on station, but the *Verbena* would not actually visit the ship until the weather broke in the spring. Thus the crew was cut off from any regular communication with land from December to May.

Writing in an era not overly preoccupied with stress, Kobbe describes the life of the crew as follows.

The emotional stress under which this crew labors can hardly be realized...The sailor on an ordinary ship has at least the inspiration of knowing that he is bound for some-where: that in due time his vessel will be laid on her homeward course; that storm and fog are but incidents of the voyage; he is on a ship that leaps forward full of life and energy with every lash of the tempest. But no matter how the lightship may plunge and roll, no matter how strong the favoring gale may be, she is still anchored two miles southeast of the New South Shoal.[12]

Despite the harsh and desolate conditions endured by the crew, their duties afforded them much free time. Each morning the lamps were lowered, cleaned, and filled, to be lighted and raised once more at dusk. Aside from daily watches and general maintenance of the ship, the intervening hours were free for the men to fill as they wished.

When they boarded the *New South Shoal* in 1856, the Nantucket crew brought with them their materials, molds, and tools for constructing "rattan" baskets. James Wood, of the legendary "row for butter," reported that when he served between 1866 and 1867 most of the men aboard were making baskets and clothespins.[13]

Baskets made aboard the *New South Shoal* rest in a sunny location a century later with two new baskets made by the author. *Collection of the Welton family.*

Basket production was still flourishing twenty-five years later, when Gustave Kobbe visited the ship.

A number of stores in Nantucket sell what are known as lightship baskets... In summer the crew occupies its spare time "scrimshawing," an old whaling term for doing ingenious mechanical work, but having aboard the *South Shoal* the special meaning (sic) of preparing the strips of wood and rattan for the manufacture of the baskets in winter. The bottoms are turned ashore. The blocks over which the baskets are made have been aboard the ship since she was first anchored off the New South Shoal in 1856. The sides of the baskets are of white oak or hickory, filled in with ratan (sic), and they are round or oval, of graceful lines and of great durability.[14]

Although Kobbe suggests that in 1891 basket bottoms were being manufactured ashore, there was a lathe on board that at other periods turned out not only basket bottoms but possibly basket molds as well.

The thirty-six years the lightship served on the South Shoals was a period of prolific basket making, as crew members constructed baskets for both family needs at home and later for shops serving the growing tourist business in Nantucket. As the "rattan baskets" began to be associated primarily with the lightship, they were referred to as "Nantucket Lightship Baskets."

Two baskets made by George Washington Ray, a relative of Captain Charles B. Ray. On the bottom of the graceful 9 1/4" oval basket is penciled "Made by George Ray aboard the lightship." Whether this was written by Mr. Ray or, as is common, a later owner/relative wishing to catalog the basket, is unknown. The round basket measurers 8 1/2". *Collection of Paul and Diane Madden.*

The hardwood rims of this 8 1/2" basket are narrow and nicely proportioned. *Collection of the Nantucket Historical Association.*

Fortunately, many of the baskets made on the lightship exist today. As the baskets were intended for service rather than decoration, sturdiness and durability were consistent characteristics. However, despite their intended use, Nantucket Lightship Baskets were extremely graceful and well-proportioned, with delicately carved handles and rims.

Baskets constructed during the lightship period were more refined than earlier rattan baskets, but their basic construction remained the same. Staves were cut primarily from white oak, hickory, and ash, using the basket makers' chief tools, a knife and drawshave. The hardwood rims of the lightship baskets were carefully fashioned in a narrow, half-round shape and were more delicate than the heavier rims of many work baskets of the period.

Unlike most lightship baskets, the handle of this beautifully proportioned 13 3/4" oval basket is fixed, extending into the body of the basket. *Collection of Paul and Diane Madden.*

Carefully carved bow handles dress up this sixteen-inch work basket. *Collection of the Welton family.*

Beautifully carved handle of old, cane-staved basket. *Private collection.*

Unlike the handles of contemporary Nantucket Lightship Baskets, which are steamed and molded, the hardwood handles of the lightship period were green wood that was tied to set its shape. The form and exquisite carving of the handles of many of these baskets are features that set off a truly lovely Nantucket Lightship Basket. Small, delicately carved "bow" handles often gave the basket a more formal look and showcased the skill of the maker.

The ears that secured the handles gave opportunity for individual creativity and a display of carving skill. Made from the same wood as the staves, the ears often extended into the slot in the basket bottom, thus serving as staves. A later more convenient but less aesthetic manner to attach the handles was the use of thin brass or tin ears that lay along the top few inches of the staves. An accompanying slot in the handle accepted the ear.

The ear of this George Folger basket is carved from the same wood as the handle and staves. *Collection of Paul and Diane Madden.*

The maker of this unfinished 6 1/2" basket was planning to carve the tops of the ears after placing them inside the basket. Today the ear would be carved completely before insertion in the baskct. *Collection of Paul and Diane Madden.*

The color of the wooden ear and handle contrasts with that of the rattan rim and staves. *Private collection.*

In both these baskets, the ear is itself a stave, inserted into the basket bottom with the other staves.

In
pe
ins
ma
pla
pe
tai
ke

Snipped tin serves as the ears on this twentieth-century basket by Ferdinand Sylvaro. *Collection of the Nantucket Historical Association.*

R. Folger, a mid-nineteenth-century basket maker who did not serve aboard the lightship, was good to those of us attempting to identify early baskets by boldly emblazoning his name on the inside of his basket bottoms.

William Appleton served aboard the *New South Shoal* under Captain Sandsbury. In the beautifully constructed eight-inch basket below, you can detect the influence of Sandsbury on his work.

Private Collection

Collection of Paul and Diane Madden

The number and pattern of lathe turnings on the basket bottoms occasionally aids in identifying a particular maker, as in the case of the Sandsbury baskets, but unfortunately it cannot be relied upon for positive identification as the number of turnings often differ with the size of each basket or even the whim of the maker.

The abundant free time aboard the lightship gave the men ample opportunity to experiment with different designs and techniques. No doubt there was some degree of competition among the men to produce a truly unique as well as finely constructed basket. From this period exist large covered baskets with brass-hinged lids, footed baskets, and baskets sporting intermittent weavers of baleen or dyed rattan.

Another experiment in design, this 8 3/4" basket is shaped like a bell. *Collection of Paul and Diane Madden.*

This unusual eight-inch basket dated 1860 is dressed with weavers of baleen, which lash the rim as well. Baleen is a flexible whalebone found in fringed plates in the mouths of right whales. The baleen, serving as a strainer, enables the whale to expel water from his mouth without losing whatever food he had taken in. *Collection of Paul and Diane Madden.*

This shallow, eleven-inch rattan-staved basket was no doubt an experiment with shape on the part of the basket maker. *Collection of Paul and Diane Madden.*

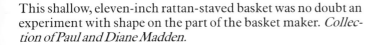

These beautifully proportioned little baskets, measuring 4 1/2" and five inches, are woven with split palm leaves. It is unusual to see such small baskets whose rims, handle, and weavers are all in proportion to the baskets' diminutive size. Note the carefully carved ear that serves also as a stave. These baskets were purchased in Nantucket in the 1860s by a Vermont couple who were "taking their wedding trip" on the island. The current owner found the honeymoon mementos still in Vermont over a century later. *Collection of Paul and Diane Madden.*

These large, lidded baskets are a unique and interesting group, estimated to have been produced between 1865 and 1885. Not many such lightship baskets are in existence today, and it is theorized that these were custom orders or perhaps special gifts to family members.

Collection of Paul and Diane Madden

By examining details of their construction, it is possible to see the manner in which the basket makers attempted to solve various problems presented them by this form.

The staves of the eleven-inch lid shown at left extend as one unit from the center to the edge. Although each is dramatically tapered, the staves still are fairly widely spaced when they reach the edge of the top. However, the staves on the 8 1/4" basket shown below begin as a single stave and split halfway out the lid in order to more tightly fill the space near the rim.

Collection of Paul and Diane Madden

Collection of Paul and Diane Madden

Collection of Paul and Diane Madden

Another problem inherent in a covered basket is how to position the handle so that the lid does not rub against it when being opened.

The ear on the basket shown at left is not set within the basket but nailed onto the outside of the rim and bent at an angle to hold the handle away from the lid. The ear on the other basket is mounted, traditionally, within the rim. However, as the ear extends above the rim, it is then bent at a right angle to prevent the lid and handle from touching. On the contemporary covered purses, ivory washers serve to butt the handle away from the rims of the basket.

45

Opposite page:
The proportions of this eleven-inch knobbed basket are especially pleasing. The handle perfectly complements the basket. Note the use of half-round rims on the basket body and flat rims on the lid.

Collection of Paul and Diane Madden

Collection of Paul and Diane Madden

Some of the lidded baskets of the period have domed lids, such as this 9 3/4" piece.

Collection of Paul and Diane Madden

Others, such as the lid of this rugged nine-inch basket, attributed to Captain Charles B. Ray, are flat.

Double-handled baskets from this period are quite rare. That this nine-inch basket is lidded makes it even more unique.

Collection of Paul and Diane Madden

The variety and quality of the baskets made aboard the *New South Shoal* are unsurpassed. The contrast between the harsh, lonely conditions endured by the lightship crew and the delicacy and grace of their baskets is striking. The many hours available to the men to perfect their designs and techniques obviously is an important reason for the baskets' beauty. However, I wonder whether creating objects of such harmony was not, at least subconsciously, a means to combat the discordant and desolate life aboard the *New South Shoal*.

Basket making aboard the ship came to a close in the early 1890s. In 1892 the ship was relocated to an even more remote station ten miles further offshore. In a notorious March blizzard that same year, the *New South Shoal* broke free of her moorings, and was driven onto No Man's Land off Martha's Vineyard. The men, half-starved and ill, were not rescued for a few weeks. The captain at that time, Andrew J. Sandsbury, retired to become the keeper of Brant Point Lighthouse on Nantucket.

The *New South Shoal* never returned to the Nantucket Shoals although she did see thirty-eight more years of service at the entrance to the Savannah River,

a testament to both her original construction and the men who cared for her for seventy-five years.

Until that time, the majority of the crew always had been Nantucketers. For some periods early in the service of the *New South Shoal*, all the crew had hailed from the island. When a new lightship, *Number 54*, was placed on the Nantucket Shoals, the composition of the crew changed radically. A letter of Mrs. Miriam Frye, daughter of Captain Sandsbury, describes her theory for this change.

My father, Captain Sandsbury, served as Mate on South Shoal Lightship for five years from 1867 to 1872, and then became her Captain... When my father retired in 1892...all the crew on the Lightship left with him, not wishing to serve under another Captain after having been so long with him. After that most of the crew were men from the mainland.[15]

As the composition of the crew changed, basket making on the Nantucket South Shoals began to come to an end. By 1905, when the last Nantucket crew member, Charles Sylvia, left lightship *Number 66*, then located on the South Shoal station, basket making was no longer conducted on the lightship.

The last lightship, *Nantucket II*, left the South Shoal Station in 1983. As was perhaps fitting to the importance of this station to coastal navigation, *Nantucket II* was the last lightship to serve in the United States. Today lightships have been replaced by unmanned large navigational buoys.

Decommissioned lightship *Number 112* anchored off Nantucket. The *112* was given to the Lightship Service in 1936 by the British government as compensation for the *117* sunk by the *Olympic* in 1934. Since her 1973 decommissioning she has served as a floating museum in both Nantucket and Portland, Maine.

Footnotes

[1] Malcolm F. Willoughby, *Lighthouses of New England* (Boston: T.O. Metcalf Co., 1929), p. 180.
[2] Edouard A. Stackpole, *Life-Saving Nantucket* (Nantucket: Stern-Majestic Press, Inc., 1972), p. 51.
[3] Willoughby, *Lighthouses of New England*, p. 181.
[4] *Ibid*
[5] Frederic L. Thompson, *The Lighthouses of Cape Cod* (Portland: Congress Square Press, 1983), p. 36.
[6] *The Boston Globe*, July 8, 1985, p. 21.
[7] George R. Putnam, *Lighthouses and Lightships of the U.S.* (Boston: Houghton Mifflin, 1917), p 210.
[8] Stackpole, *Life-Saving Nantucket*, p. 68.

[9] Putnam, *Lighthouses*, p. 210.
[10] Stackpole, *Life-Saving Nantucket*, p 65.
[11] *Ibid.*, p. 66.
[12] Gustave Kobbe, "Life on the South Shoal Lightship" as reprinted in Frederic Thompson's *The Lightships of Cape Cod*, p. 110.
[13] Everett U. Crosby, *Signs and Silver of Old Time Nantucket* (Nantucket: Inquirer and Mirror Press, 1940), p. 68.
[14] Kobbe, "Life on the South Shoal Lightship," p. 109.
[15] Stackpole, *Life-Saving Nantucket*, p. 68.

The town of Nantucket, viewed from across the harbor at Monomoy.

This seven-inch island-made basket was constructed by Oliver Coffin, "formerly of South Shoal Lightship." *Collection of the Nantucket Historical Association.*

Chapter 3
Nantucket-Made Baskets

During the fifty years of basket making at sea, the craft continued on Nantucket. Some makers were retired crew, others never had served on the lightship at all. Like their counterparts aboard the *New South Shoal*, island basket makers supplied the needs of both family and retail shops.

In 1929 Mary Eliza Starbuck wrote about her girlhood on Nantucket. Entitled *My House and I*, her book gives not only a delightful account of nineteenth-century island life, but also refers to Nantucket Lightship Baskets.

Early in Miss Starbuck's life, her widowed mother married James Wyer, captain of the whale ship *Spartan*. Captain Wyer filled his spare time constructing baskets, a "labor of love" according to his stepdaughter.

His baskets were beautifully made, and all our friends were fitted out with little workbaskets, or egg baskets, and sometimes he would make the whole nest of seven for some favorite among the many young people who came to our home.[1]

Captain James Wyer. *Collection of the Nantucket Historical Association.*

The smallest of Captain Wyer's nest, measuring 5 1/2", is woven with proportionally finer cane. The staves, rim, and handle also mirror the smallest size. The largest basket in this nest is 12 3/8". Note the elaborate carving on each handle. *Collection of the Nantucket Historical Association.*

Although Miss Starbuck describes her stepfather's "nest of seven," this nest appears to be missing a basket which, if present, would make a total of eight baskets. *Collection of the Nantucket Historical Association.*

In another reference Miss Starbuck recalls Sunday morning outings to cut roses at her stepfather's "old" house on Orange Street.

He always carried a shallow rattan basket, the sort known as "lightship baskets," but in those days almost any seafaring man could and did make them. Stepfather's were beautifully made. He wasn't as original in his ideas as Father, he always had to have a pattern, but his work, equally accurate with Father's, was more delicately finished.[2]

Captain Wyer's choice of narrow rattan staves and delicately carved handle for this shallow 9 3/4" basket reflect his stepdaughter's description of his work. *Collection of the Nantucket Historical Association.*

A twentieth-century Orange Street doorway.

Elaborate lathe turnings grace the inside of the Wyer basket. *Collection of Nantucket Historical Association.*

Written on the bottom of the basket is "M.E. Starbuck, January 28, 1880, Made by James Wyer. January, 1877." *Collection of the Nantucket Historical Association.*

Although basket making ceased on the lightship by the turn of the century, the craft continued on the island. Early twentieth century basket makers often had either served aboard the lightship or had been taught basketry by former crew members. William Appleton had made baskets aboard the *New South Shoal* and later kept a basket shop on lower Orange Street until about 1910. Those of his baskets that were actually made on the lightship are labeled "Made aboard the *New South Shoal*." Others show his name and "Nantucket, Mass."

This William Appleton basket was constructed at his home on Orange Street. Note the turning on the bottom's edge. *Collection of Paul and Diane Madden.*

LIGHTSHIP
BASKET
Made by
WILLIAM E. APPLETON,
NANTUCKET, MASS.

Appleton in turn taught A.D. Williams of 120 Orange Street, who produced boldly signed baskets in the 1910s and 1920s. It is assumed that Williams instructed his neighbor, Ferdinand Sylvaro, of 97 Orange Street, who continued the work through the 1920s and 1930s. Many of both Williams' and Sylvaro's baskets survive today.

According to one visitor to Sylvaro's "orderly" workshop attached to his home, many of Sylvaro's baskets were being made on molds that had belonged to Davis Hall of the *New South Shoal*.[3] The value of the basket maker's mold, especially the lovely ones crafted on the lightship, is evidenced by this passing on of molds from one maker to another. In fact old Nantucket Lightship Basket molds are as desired by some contemporary collectors as the antique baskets themselves.

Lower Orange Street, the site of much basket making in the early twentieth century, as it appears today.

This unusual eleven-inch shallow basket, whose carved staves extend over the rim, is attributed to Ferdinand Sylvaro. It is constructed with far more care and detail than his basket at the bottom of the following page, illustrating the wide range of quality that can be found within the work of one basket maker. *Collection of Paul and Diane Madden.*

An eight-inch oval by A.D. Williams, dated August 11, 1926. *Collection of the Nantucket Historical Association.*

The handle of this round basket by Ferdinand Sylvaro is very similar to that carved by his neighbor, A.D. Williams. *Collection of the Nantucket Historical Association.*

55

An informative little three-inch basket gives the history of its maker, "Made by Elijah Alley (came from Lynn to Nantucket), m. Mary Burdick." *Collection of the Nantucket Historical Association.*

Perhaps the most well-known basket maker of the post-lightship period was Mitchell (Mitchy) Ray. He inherited his craft from his grandfather and father, both makers before him. His grandfather, Captain Charles B. Ray, was descended fittingly enough from a family of coopers and learned basketry from Captain Thomas James of the *New South Shoal*. In 1866 Captain Ray informed Nantucket's newspaper, *The Inquirer and Mirror*, that he had just completed his two hundredth basket, 140 of which he had sold.

Seated at the same shaving horse as his father and grandfather, Mitchy Ray turned out many baskets in the 1920s, 1930s, and 1940s. Apparently as prolific as his grandfather, in the fall of 1946 he had 200 orders that he planned to fill during the following winter at his unhurried but steady pace.

"This, I suppose," he dryly told a 1945 interviewer, "might be called an old established business."

My father worked at it and my grandfather so this isn't what you would call a new thing... I have made baskets to go to every state in the Union and outside the country too... That's what comes from making things right, no cuttin' corners.[4]

His sturdy, square-handled baskets were durable constructions. To many of Ray's baskets are still attached the verse he included with each one.

I was made on Nantucket
I'm strong and I'm stout.
Don't lose me or burn me,
And I'll never wear out.

These "stout" baskets apparently were created in a setting of organized chaos. Unlike Sylvaro's orderly work place,

the most extraordinary feature of this shop was the collection of solid wood basket forms inherited in part from Captain Ray. They were strewn all about the shop, on the floor, piled on shelves, and in the open loft, perhaps a hundred all told, looking like weathered tops of giant mushrooms.[5]

One visitor marveled that Ray could ever find anything in the disorder!

Despite Ray's productivity, Nantucket Lightship Basket making was considered to be a "dying art" by the 1930s. We can be grateful to

Mitchell Ray at work. *Collection of Nantucket Historical Association.*

This sturdy 15 1/4" oval work basket by Mitchell Ray carries his characteristic "squared" handle and 3/8" wide staves. *Collection of the Nantucket Historical Association.*

These three-inch, one-egg baskets signed by Mitchell Ray, though charming, suggest he perhaps was more comfortable working on a larger scale. *Collection of the Nantucket Historical Association.*

Mitchy Ray for keeping the craft alive. Charging modest prices averaging $5.00 per basket and suffering hindrances such as World War II rattan shortages, Ray nevertheless continued what must have been a labor of love. In an interview in the mid-1940s, he expressed regret that as a seventy-six-year-old bachelor he had no one to whom to pass on his three generations of knowledge.

Fortunately Ray kept at his work and his desire to pass on his craft was soon realized in a new friendship with the man who was to be responsible for the resurgence of the basket's fame.

Footnotes

[1] Mary Eliza Starbuck, *My House and I* (Boston: Houghton Mifflin, 1929), p. 238.
[2] *Ibid.*, p. 117.
[3] Allen H. Eaton, *Handicrafts of New England* (New York: Bonanza Books, 1949), p. 60.
[4] Art McGinley, "*A Personal Chat with a Nantucket Basket Maker*," *The Inquirer and Mirror*, September 29, 1945.
[5] Eaton, *Handicrafts of New England*, p. 59.

Note the carefully chamfered edges of each hickory stave. *Collection of the Nantucket Historical Association.*

José Formoso Reyes at work in his crowded shop. *Collection of the Nantucket Historical Association.*

Signature of Mr. Reyes.

60

Chapter 4
José Reyes Baskets

Unlike Mitchell Ray, the man so important to the future of the Nantucket Lightship Basket was not a third or even second generation Nantucket basket maker. In fact, at his birth in 1902, José Reyes lived half a world away in a small Philippine village in Ilocos Sur Province. The oldest of ten children of a self-educated Methodist minister, José Reyes was reared in an atmosphere of hard work and reverence for learning. Like the other village children, he was taught to make baskets as soon as he could hold a knife. Pride in careful craftsmanship was emphasized. In addition to weaving the actual basket, the young Reyes learned from his father how to process the rattan that they harvested themselves from the jungle. Rattan, an important material in the villages, was used for baskets, mats, fencing, and even tying houses together.

An interesting sequence of events led José Reyes to become a part of the story of Nantucket Lightship Baskets. Desiring to expand on the education he had received in his village school, he came to the United States and attended high school in Portland, Oregon. Supporting himself with a variety of jobs, he graduated with honors and went on to Reed College. His successful career at Reed won him a scholarship for graduate study at Harvard and also paired him in a long marriage to a Massachusetts woman.

Reyes received his Masters in Education in 1932. The Reyes's returned to the Philippines where Mr. Reyes taught English at the University of the Philippines and later headed the Department of Languages and Social Arts at the Philippine Military Academy. World War II interrupted this life, however, and Lt. Reyes was transferred to the staff of the U.S. Army General Command Headquarters in Manila. He saw action in Battan before its fall and was sent underground to organize resistance and maintain contact with American forces.

The first basket, a nine-inch oval, made by Mr. Reyes after settling on Nantucket. Two pieces of plywood were nailed together as a base. The edges of the plywood were then covered with a piece of cane. *Collection of the Nantucket Historical Association.*

The antecedent of the Friendship Basket, this was Mr. Reyes's first covered basket. It measures 5 3/4". Although he used a solid piece of wood for the base, he had yet to incorporate a wooden plate in the basket's lid. The ingenious handle placement would later change to a more traditional one. *Collection of the Nantucket Historical Association.*

The bottom of this first covered basket is signed in the manner that would be used in all Reyes baskets. Around an outline map of Nantucket is printed, "Made in Nantucket...José Formoso Reyes." *Collection of Nantucket Historical Association.*

After the liberation of the Philippines in 1945, Mr. Reyes accompanied his war-weakened family on a refugee ship to Los Angeles. From there the family was transported to Boston and on to Nantucket for a recuperative vacation at the summer home of Mrs. Reyes's mother. Attracted to the peace and subtle beauty of the island, the Reyes family decided to make it their home. Frustrated in his search for a teaching position in the Nantucket schools, Reyes turned to house painting and supplemented his income by repairing cane and rush chairs.

At this point he became friends with Mitchell Ray, who encouraged him to bring his native basketry ability to the craft of the Nantucket Lightship Basket. Under Ray's tutelage and using many of Ray's old molds, Reyes began what would be his new career. His active mind soon came up with the idea for a covered basket to be used as a lady's purse. A few of these baskets, woven in the summer of 1948, sold "like hotcakes" according to their weaver. So many orders poured in that Reyes turned to basket making as a full-time occupation.

For the staves of his baskets, Reyes chose to employ rattan, the material so familiar to him from boyhood. To differentiate his rattan-staved covered baskets from traditional open wooden-staved ones, he dubbed them "Friendship Baskets" for their ability to initiate conversations when spotted by Nantucket aficionados in far-flung corners of the world. However, in a 1960 conversation taped for the Nantucket Historical Association, Mr. Reyes made a point of noting that many of the "old, old" baskets he had seen carried rattan staves, perhaps politely implying that indeed his baskets were a legitimate part of the long tradition of Nantucket Lightship Baskets.

The idea for ornamenting Reyes's covered baskets with ivory or ebony whales followed quickly, and the ornamentation became as varied as the shapes and sizes of the baskets emanating from his small, cluttered York Street workshop. Amid hanging bundles of rattan, baskets in progress, and drying handles, Mr. Reyes quietly worked long days investing each basket with his skill and pride as a craftsman. Like his mentor, Mitchy Ray, José Reyes chose to spend time with each basket rather than to succumb to the opportunities offered him to churn out more product for greater monetary reward. A treasured personal memory is ordering my first basket in 1968 as Mr. Reyes patiently explained the options available. Did I like this basket with the flared sides? Would I prefer a basket woven higher or lower? Each basket was, without doubt, individually designed.

A late 1940s six-inch round basket still carries its Reyes signature. Unfortunately, many signatures have worn off over the years. *Private collection.*

Ebony whales were the first to adorn the tops of Reyes's baskets. These three early examples of his work exemplify not only the lovely proportions characteristic of his baskets, but also the rich patina most Reyes baskets have acquired over the years. *Private collection.*

This seven-inch basket has had many years of use since Mr. Reyes made it in the late 1940s. It originally featured a leather shoulder strap that was later converted to a wooden handle. *Private collection.*

Made in 1954, this eight-inch oval was adorned with an ivory seagull. *Private collection.*

A mellow patina and attractive shape characterize this early 1950s seven-inch oval. *Collection of Claudia Gordon.*

To hold the handle away from the opening basket lid, Mr. Reyes inserted a long piece of turned ivory through the handle and into the basket rim. Later handles were set off by washers, as is common today. *Private collection.*

This seven-inch basket made in 1963 was not woven as high as most of Mr. Reyes's baskets. *Collection of Wendy Lawrence.*

An unusually shaped rectangular double-handled basket dating from the 1950s. *Collection of Paul and Diane Madden.*

Decorating the top of this charming eight-inch basket made by Mr. Reyes in 1962 is the map of Nantucket carved by Nancy Chase. The handle is beautifully shaped and the basket has a rich, warm, patina. *Private collection.*

In 1980, a few months before his death, Mr. Reyes estimated that he had constructed over 5,000 baskets that had found homes all over the world. Among the many well-known women who could claim ownership of a Reyes basket was Queen Elizabeth II, who was presented with one at her coronation in 1953.

It was not the number or even the quality of José Reyes's baskets, however, that remain his most important contribution to the craft. Rather, the popularity and renown of his work renewed interest in the Nantucket Lightship Basket and rekindled appreciation of the existing baskets of earlier eras. José Reyes was truly the answer to Mitchy Ray's concern that the craft would be forgotten. In the NHA interview of 1960, Mr. Reyes's soft voice modestly acknowledged his contribution to the basket's history.

Ever since I've started to make these baskets...I've always felt that...I am contributing to something that Nantucket has originated and it makes me feel good...There's nothing more beautiful than the lightship basket to me, and I've known baskets all my life...The simplicity of the lightship basket contributes to its beauty. It is constructed so strongly...so sturdily. It seems to me that Nantucket has something it should be proud of in these baskets. It...makes me proud because I can contribute to perpetuating a Nantucket art that should not be lost, that should keep going on forever.

This six-inch basket, dating from the 1960s, originally had carved ivory water skis decorating its wooden lid. *Collection of Barbara Lawrence.*

These scrimshawed "quarterboards" serve as both identification and ornamentation inside the lids of their respective Reyes baskets. Although all the baskets themselves have filler pieces to cover the space between the inner and outer rims, only some of the lids are constructed in this manner. *Private collection.*

This sturdy nine-inch honey-colored basket was made by
Sherman Boyer, probably in the 1950s. *Private collection.*

Today neither Ray nor Reyes need fear the death of the craft. Many basket makers both on and off Nantucket are constructing Lightship Baskets with varying degrees of proficiency. As competition has increased more attention has been given to finessing the baskets. Except for a few other makers such as Sherman Boyer, Stephen Gibbs, and Stanley Roop, José Reyes was essentially *the* Nantucket Lightship Basket maker of the 1950s and 1960s.

In this detail view of another Boyer basket, note the closely spaced, heavy oak staves and sturdy handle. Made in the 1950s, this nine-inch basket will give many more years of service. *Private collection.*

Boyer often used the same ditty as did Mitchy Ray when labeling his baskets. *Private collection.*

However, as basket prices increased and more craftsmen entered the field in the 1970s and 1980s, each attempted to differentiate his work from that of his competitors. Only so much innovation can be performed on a basket whose weave and materials already are proscribed. Thus makers began to give attention to finer details. A great number of staves and finer weavers were used to create a tighter, more delicate weave, and more attention was given to precision shaping of molds so that tops, bottoms, and rims of baskets matched perfectly. Further serving to showcase the talents of individual craftsmen was the imaginative incorporation of exotic woods and ivory, new molds of non-traditional shapes, and a variety of baskets ingeniously designed for service as cradles, ice buckets, and tables.

Compared to many highly ornamented contemporary baskets, a well-used, gracefully proportioned Reyes basket appears refreshingly ingenuous. Although the trend for refinement has resulted in exquisite baskets, there is undeniably a quiet charm and personality to those baskets constructed in a simpler, less competitive era.

Antique
come highly
tory, and in
kets still per
the harmon
mellow pati
play alone.

We can s
the *New Sc*
amounts cha
credulous at
lightship bas
and apprecia
fiance decide
place the "rat
gone with t
"antiquers" l
ing for a few
some Nantuc
tique baskets

Even tho
baskets often
of the Folger
bers its year
grandmother
keys or whate
There are ma
baskets in har
or gathering
Before being 1
workbasket o
a small shed,
cozy home fo

Surprising
years of servi
which is so h
kets carefully
are not favore
hard-working

PRICE LIST
(Subject to revision without notice)

Baskets

Oval	Large	9 in. x 7 1/2 in. x 6 in.	$50.00
Oval	Medium	8 1/2 in. x 6 1/2 in. x 5 in.	$45.00
Oval	Medium	8 in. x 6 in. x 5 in.	$40.00 (small)
Oval	Small	7 1/2 in. x 5 in. x 4 1/2 in.	$35.00
Round	Large	9 inches diameter	$40.00
Round	Small	8 inches diameter	$35.00

Special sizes and shapes made to order:
Long ovals, Diamond shape, Square, Rectangular, Creel, and Half-round.

Ivory Carvings

Whale in ivory (miniature) Regular size	$14.00
(Same prices fro ebony whales) Larger sizes	$18.00-$25.00
Sea gulls in ivory (depending upon size)	$30.00-$50.00

Any special carvings can be made upon request, such as: sea horses, whales, birds of any kind.

Ivory Fittings

Ivory catches	$18.00 each
Ivory pegs	$3.00 each

(Same price for ebony fittings)

Plaques

Ebony	$10.00-$20.00
Ivory	$22.00-$60.00
Mahogany	$10.00-$20.00

Price list of Reyes baskets dating from the 1950s.

Opposite:
Copper pots and
this kitchen.

When evaluating an antique lightship basket, a rich patina, good condition, and features such as delicate rims and handles all are elements to consider. Repaired baskets should be identified as such. Finally, as when purchasing a new piece, attention to construction details is important. There can be a wide range of quality even within the work of one maker. Perhaps his early baskets were not as refined as subsequent ones; or, conversely, lack of competition in his later years might have caused the quality to slip. It also is helpful to be able to roughly estimate the age of the basket, as its purported age may be a factor in its pricing. The following clues to determining age are included as guidelines only, as there are likely to be exceptions to any rule.

A Ruth Congdon oil painting revealing the view from Nantucket's Steamboat Wharf as it appeared in the 1940s provides a fitting backdrop for these old baskets.

Nantucket simplicity.

A rich color and patina is not only desirable aesthetically but also may indicate the relative age of a basket. Generally the darker the color, the older the basket. However, as mentioned, well-used baskets may have darker coloring than older, more protected ones. Occasionally you may find a lightship basket that has been unscrupulously stained to lend an "aged" appearance.

Nails fastening the rim also can serve as clues to age. Earlier nineteenth century baskets were nailed with iron or copper nails, whereas brass nails became more common toward the turn of the century.

Handles of earlier nineteenth century baskets usually were attached by means of ears that extended down into the basket. The ears of older baskets were carved of wood, whereas a brass or tin ear would place the age of a basket in at least the latter part of the nineteenth century.

A basket whose base is comprised of two pieces of wood nailed together would be considered a very early lightship basket. In addition, baskets of this period might well carry thin staves of wooden splint rather than the thicker staves later produced with spokeshaves. Staves shaved in this way often vary in thickness, whereas earlier splint staves and later, contemporary saw-cut staves are more uniform.

If the basket has cane staves, examination of the staves may give a clue to age. Cane staves of early baskets usually were cut from slab rattan and were of irregular thickness. Most of these baskets are believed to have been made between 1850 and 1870, the period written about by Joseph Farnham. However, stray rattan-staved baskets are scattered throughout the nineteenth century. Staves of more uniformly cut cane would be found in twentieth century baskets.

The detective work involved can be enjoyable and can lead to greater appreciation of the work of different basket makers. Curious to see if the small, unidentified six-inch basket illustrated at left might possibly be the work of R. Folger, a collector and I brought together two Folger baskets, both from different collections, to compare them to the unidentified basket.

The first discovery was that the two Folger baskets(six inches and seven inches) nested together perfectly and, if not part of the same nest, were undoubtedly made on molds that had been constructed to form part of a nest.

As for the unidentified basket, there certainly were some similarities to the Folger baskets. The criss-cross lashing viewed from the top of the basket (as seen at the bottom of page 78), as well as the manner in which the lashing travelled around the basket ear, (as seen in the top photo, this page) was identical.

The shapes of the baskets were similar, as were the widths of the wooden staves. However, the ear of the unidentified basket (in the middle) was taller than the other two, the handle carving dissimilar, and the rims were thicker and flatter than the Folger baskets.

Finally, the bottom of the unidentified basket was carved while the bottoms of the Folger baskets were left straight-sided. (Bottom right photo)

The verdict of the expert in attendance? Probably not a Folger. However, R. Folger could have been experimenting with carved bottoms, taller ears, and flatter rims on earlier baskets before he discovered the style he preferred as represented in the two identified baskets! Delving into the motives of someone working over a hundred years ago is an imprecise science at best. As we studiously review the shape of each handle, we only can imagine with dread the men aboard the lightship borrowing handles from each other and insuring confusion a century later!

Old lightship baskets, like other wooden antiques, should be maintained in an atmosphere that is properly humidified. The mantle of a working fireplace is not the spot to display your antique! A coat of oil sprayed or brushed on can help prevent dryness. When broken weavers are so dry that they are crumbling, a basket can be shellacked to literally hold it together.

Although antique baskets can be repaired, knowledgeable collectors and dealers believe it is preferable to avoid or minimize repairs in order to maintain value and to prevent further damage by invading the basket. However, if the basket is so damaged that it has little monetary value, or if it is a working basket the owner wishes to have in serviceable order once more, repairs are then indicated.

The original lashing of this 11 1/2" basket was executed in a criss-cross pattern, as can be seen by the marks left on the rim. The repaired lashing appears awkward not only because of the lighter shade of the new cane but also because it did not faithfully follow the original pattern. *Collection of the Nantucket Historical Association.*

Collection of the Welton family

Collection of the Welton family

The colors of these new baskets made by the author contrast sharply with the patina acquired over the years, evident in the antique baskets. *Collection of the Welton family.*

Chapter 6
Contemporary Baskets

The purpose of creating a Nantucket Lightship Basket has changed considerably over the years. In the nineteenth century, this basket was a utilitarian object intended for a life of service. Its shape, wooden bottom, and ability to be nested were all conceived to fulfill certain functions. However, the fine manufacture of the nineteenth century basket makers and their attention to detail, balance, and form resulted in their work being valued more for its beauty than function.

In contrast, contemporary baskets are designed primarily for appearance and only secondarily to serve utilitarian functions. Perhaps the greatest change in the history of the lightship basket is this change in intent. However, today's baskets are crafted as durably as those made one hundred years ago and can offer the potential for as much service as their ancestors. Contemporary basket makers share with their nineteenth century predecessors a commitment to the craft.

The following photographs illustrate work by contemporary basket makers Judy and Bill Sayle, Bob and Karen Marks of "Oak and Ivory;" Alan S.W. Reed, Nap Plank, and Janet Bowman of "Nantucket Basket Works"; and the author. These basket makers represent a small sampling of the many fine craftsmen also creating beautifully constructed Nantucket Lightship Baskets, but whose work is not included here.

Contemporary handbags are designed individually to reflect the owner's personality, style, or experiences. Carvings and scrimshaw decorating the baskets of José Reyes often had nautical themes, celebrating Nantucket's whaling days. Whales and ships remain favorites as illustrated in the baskets to follow.

Ebony sperm whales adorn this ivory-topped nine-inch basket by Bob and Karen Marks. The ebony theme is continued in the knobs and peg. An overlay of ivory decorates the handle. Ebony carving by Al Doucette. (Photo by Deborah Donovan.)

Mother and baby dolphin, carved by Al Doucette, frolic on the Purple Heart top of this eight-inch basket by the author.

Opposite:
The nest of seven baskets by Bob and Karen Marks ranges in size from seven to sixteen inches. (Photo by Deborah Donovan.)

An ivory schooner carved by Al Doucette graces the lid of this eight inch basket crafted by the author.

Humpback whales, mother and calf, give personality to this eight-inch oval purse by the author. Ivory carving by Al Doucette.

To commemorate the many happy hours sailing my "beetle cat" in Nantucket Harbor, I chose this carving by Al Doucette to top this eight-inch basket.

The nautical theme could find no finer execution than in this exquisite six-inch "Sailor Boy" basket by Alan S.W. Reed. Scrimshaw by Lee A. Papale. (Photo by Jack Weinhold.)

Nantucket Lightship baskets, made by Bill and Judy Sayle, sit in the shadow of lightship *Number 112*, serving at the time as a floating museum. (Photo by Marshall DuBock).

The nine-inch basket by Nap Plank has a turned wooden lid, ivory overlay on the handle, and an ivory knob scrimmed by Lee A. Papale. (Photo by Jack Weinhold)

The beautiful lines and symmetry of shells make them favorite images to reproduce in carving and scrimshaw.

A horseshoe crab, starfish, sand dollar, quahog, scallop, conch, and soft-shelled clam adorn the ivory lid of the seven-inch cocktail basket by Bob and Karen Marks. (Cocktail baskets are so dubbed because they are smaller and often fancier "party" baskets as distinguished from "everyday" lightship baskets. Carvings by Al Doucette. Photo by Deborah Donovan.)

The classic symmetry of a scallop shell perfectly complements the form of a Nantucket Lightship Basket. Eight-inch ivory-topped basket by the author, shell carved by Al Doucette, clasp by David Brown.

In an unusual treatment, whalebone is inlaid in rosewood and topped with a whalebone scallop shell. Knobs and pegs are also whalebone. Eight-inch basket by the author. Carving by Charles A. Manghis.

Double scallop shells are surrounded by delicately colored beach flowers on this seven-inch cocktail basket by Bob and Karen Marks. Shell carving by Al Doucette, scrimshaw by David Smith. (Photo by Deborah Donovan.)

Treasured scenes or favorite flowers have become preferred ways to personalize a basket.

Tiger lilies abound on this 7 1/2" cocktail basket by Alan S.W. Reed. Scrimshander Lee A. Papale has even scrimmed the handle knobs with the lilies. (Photo by Jack Weinhold.)

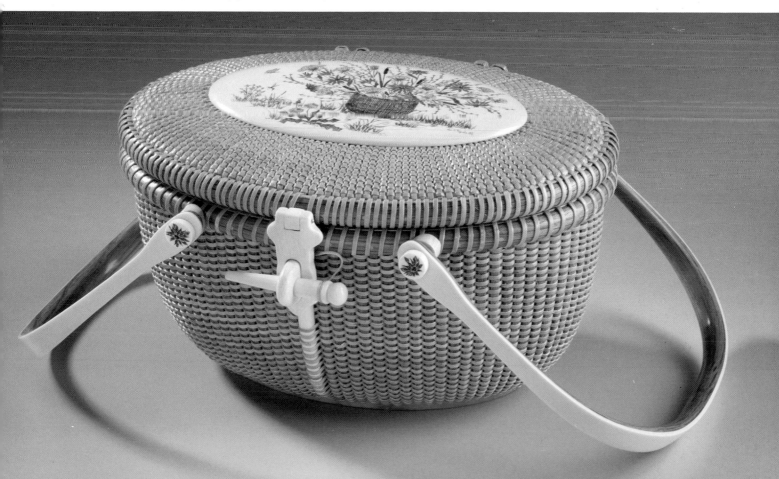

This eight-inch basket by the author nestles in the dune grass in view of the scene that inspired it - North Light, Block Island, Rhode Island. Scrimshaw by M.H. Whelan.

As the owner of this classic eight-inch basket resides in Barbados, she chose tropical hibiscus as well as her monogram to personalize her bag. Basket by the author. Scrimshaw by Charles A. Manghis.

This handsome ten-inch basket by Bob and Karen Marks carries double handles of walnut. Complementing the colors is the sepia scrimshaw of sandpipers by David Smith. (Photo by Deborah Donovan.)

Not all contemporary baskets fulfill strictly decorative roles, as demonstrated by the following examples.

Eight-inch ice bucket by Bob and Karen Marks has a turned cherry top knobbed with ivory. (Photo by Deborah Donovan.)

What baby could want a more finely crafted cradle than this thirty-five-inch-long cherry piece by Bob and Karen Marks? (Photo by Deborah Donovan.)

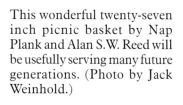

This wonderful twenty-seven inch picnic basket by Nap Plank and Alan S.W. Reed will be usefully serving many future generations. (Photo by Jack Weinhold.)

Nantucket Lightship Baskets can prove both useful and decorative, as evidenced in these happy scenes from a June wedding on Martha's Vineyard. These six-inch baskets were made by the author.

In fact, Nantucket Lightship Baskets can elegantly hold flowers, eggs, or bunnies...

Baskets made by the author.

...or simply be appreciated for their own beauty.

Opposite page: A converted hat mold from a Nantucket milliner was the basis for this classic, shallow twelve-inch basket by Nap Plank. Scrimshaw by Lee A. Papale. (Photo by Jack Weinhold.)

Solomon's seal provides the backdrop for this six-inch basket by the author.

This nineteen-inch oval hearth basket by the author appears fittingly placed beside the Atlantic.

Opposite page: Although each basket is staved with a different material, both this basket and the Marks' basket shown on page 98 are beautifully constructed and correspond to the guidelines outlined for purchasing a new Nantucket Lightship Basket. This easy-to-carry seven-inch shoulder bag by Janet Bowman is staved with cane. Its ivory top is scrimmed with a beach scene by Lee A. Papale (Photo by Jack Weinhold.)

This cherry-lidded oak basket is a relatively recent hybrid that blends elements of a traditional lightship basket with those of a fishing creel.

This collection of baskets made by the author range in size from three to twenty four inches and testify to the impact a grouping can make in a decorating scheme.

Although commitment to craftsmanship has remained constant throughout the years, the purchase price of a Nantucket Lightship Basket has changed undeniably.

After investing in a contemporary basket, many new owners understandably are hesitant to give the basket the use it can take. However, even a new basket will mellow and "age" more quickly and attractively if lovingly used. Obviously there is a difference between use and abuse, but a Nantucket Lightship Basket is a sturdy creation capable of a life of service.

When investing in a new basket or beginning to collect older versions, try to be aware of points that will help you better evaluate your choices. For new work, it is both interesting and informative to go, if possible, directly to one or more basket makers. Although you now can find basket makers both on and off Nantucket, select one whose island training or associations can assure you that you are dealing with someone who constructs the basket in the traditional manner. They will be able to point out qualities that they strive to incorporate in their work and also can "design" for you a customized basket whose shape, woods, and types of ornamentation please you. Furthermore, they will be able to make the minor repairs your basket will require over the years. Common repairs include mending broken weavers and rim lashing and replacing the leather hinges of purses. However, with the help of a skilled basket maker, a Nantucket Lightship Basket can recover from even more serious injuries, including broken staves and cracked rims.

The eight-inch handbag by Bob and Karen Marks is staved with oak, as are all their baskets. The shell scrimshaw by David Smith is mounted on a lustrous top of Goncalo Alves. (Photo by Deborah Donovan.)

If you are unable to visit the actual basket maker, there do exist specialized shops whose owners carry the work of a few selected basket makers. In a quality shop, the personnel should not only be familiar with the construction of Nantucket Lightship Baskets in general, but also should be able to point out differences between the work of one basket maker and another to aid you in your decision.

Never purchase an "imitation" lightship basket whose maker is unknown and whose price seems too good to be true. These baskets are poorly made, imported to the United States for a few dollars, often stained for a quickly "aged" look, and frequently sell for well over one hundred dollars. They have no present or future value and cannot easily be repaired. A good leather purse would be an infinitely wiser investment of your cash!

When selecting a basket, you must decide whether you wish one that is staved with cane or oak. Advocates of oak staves, which are more time-consuming to prepare, invoke both the durability of oak and its undeniable place in the tradition of lightship baskets. Those who prefer cane not only appreciate the delicate look it lends to a basket but also believe it to be more resilient than oak and thus more likely to bounce back from abuse. Other basket makers, believing the difference to be a "matter of aesthetics," work in both mediums.

There are other details to be aware of in making your choice. Look for staves that are straight and evenly spaced, a nice tight weave in which no holes appear, weavers that flow evenly over and under each stave without any dips or waves, a well-formed and attractively lashed rim, and a carefully carved handle whose design appears to complement the basket. If choosing a purse, ascertain that the top is well matched and fitted to the bottom and that the leather hinges are attractively and securely inserted.

Personalization even can include one's profession. For this eight-inch purse, Charles A. Manghis scrimmed a group of my baskets overlooking the ocean. The ivory latch was carved by David Brown.

This nest of eight baskets made by the author range in size from three to twelve inches.

SUPPLIES LIST

Materials:	Tools:
Basket mold	Sharp utility knife
Basket base	Three or four various width screwdrivers
Handle	Fine grade sandpaper
Number 20 escutcheon pins for rim	Pliers
Numbr 14 Escutcheon pins or rivet for handle	Large rubber band
Copper washers/burrs	Rule or tape measure
Ivory knobs (optional)	Utility scissors
Stave material: six-millimeter-wide binding cane, or milled oak	Wire cutters
Weaver: carriage fine cane	Pencil
Filler piece: common cane	Plane
Rims: 3/8" half-round reed	Cyanoacrylate (or fast-drying) glue
Base plug: 1/4"dowel	Clothes pins or clamps
	Hobby drill and bits
	Ballpeen hammer
	Clear shellac or polyurethane
	Brush
	Small saw

Chapter 7
Construction

Basket molds of differing shapes and sizes.

To create your own Nantucket Lightship Basket in the traditional manner is a challenging but wonderfully rewarding project. In addition to the concrete reward of the finished basket, you will be able to better appreciate and evaluate other lightship baskets once you actually have constructed one yourself.

Until recently, however, a Nantucket Lightship Basket could be constructed only by those skilled enough to turn out their own wooden molds, bases, and handles. To create a mold requires much patience, knowledge of wood, and woodworking skill. The mold is the basis of all the baskets produced on it. When the mold is created, the shape of one or perhaps hundreds of baskets is then decided. Unlike free-formed baskets made without molds, the mold, not the tension of the weaver, determines the shape of the Nantucket Lightship Basket.

Basket makers expend great effort to assure that their wooden mold will have a pleasing shape and proportion, as it will become the maker's "signature." To construct a round mold, layers of wood are glued together and then cut in a cylindrical shape whose diameter is slightly larger than that planned for the finished mold.

The wood cylinder then is turned on a wood lathe until the mold reaches the proper diameter and the desired shape. Some round molds have very abrupt curves, while others curve more gradually. I prefer a softer, more gradual curve although this shape takes longer to achieve as more wood has to be removed. Shape preference is just that-a preference, a personal taste. There is no "right" or "wrong" look.

An oval mold begins in the same way as a round mold. Layers of wood are glued together and then cut into an oval shape. The rough shaping of the curve can be accomplished mechanically. However, the final fashioning must be done by hand. This time-consuming process involves not only creating an attractively shaped curve, but also insuring that the arc of the curve is consistent around the bottom of the mold.

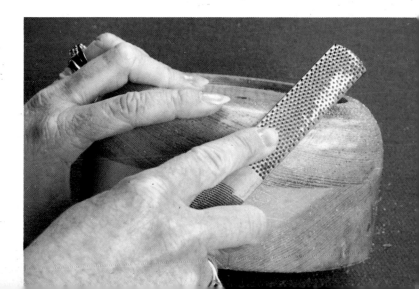

Shaping the curve of an oval mold.

Round and oval rim molds, 3/8" half-rounded reed for rims.

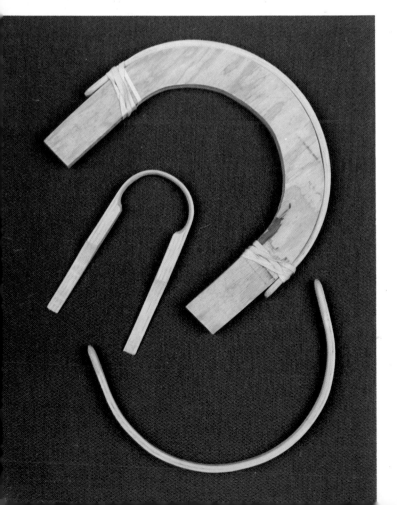

Standard swing handle and its mold, bent "side" handles available from basketry supply houses.

I enjoy shaping the mold, running my hands over the curve to detect imperfections. The true test of the mold, however, is the first basket made on it. I often have "finished" an oval mold only to have all its flaws made very obvious by the shape of the basket it produces. After examining the basket, I then can refine the mold to eliminate its flaws.

Although constructing a mold can bring much satisfaction, not everyone has the tools, skills, or even the desire to accomplish this. Recently some basketry supply houses have begun producing lines of "Nantucket" supplies (molds, bases, and handles) enabling those unskilled in woodworking to nevertheless experience the pleasure of making their *own* Nantucket Lightship Baskets.

The following instructions for making a round Nantucket Lightship Basket will assume that you either have made or purchased a basket mold, rim mold, wooden base, and handle.

As it is so readily available, you may choose to use cane (rattan) for both the weaver and the staves. However, if you have access to oak, you may wish to use that for the staves and rims. The following photographs actually will illustrate three baskets under construction. One will have staves of cane; the second will have oak splint staves; and the third will have staves of thicker milled oak. Oak staves will require more preparation than cane. You will want to sand the sides of each stave to round the edges. The manner in which the cane is cut commercially lends a softened appearance to the edges of the cane without further preparation by the basket maker. You also may have to adjust the number of staves in the basket if the oak staves are wider (or narrower) than the six-millimeter staves used in this example.

The mold illustrated is a round, seven-inch mold. The wooden base is 3 7/8" in diameter. However, not all seven-inch molds take similarly sized bases. The diameter of a base can vary greatly from mold to mold. Thus, when ordering a base, specify the exact diameter of the base rather than the diameter of the mold.

The staves of this basket are cane. It is woven with super-fine cane and rimmed with reed.

Both the staves and the rims of these three baskets are oak.

Preparing the Base

1. Wooden bases usually are shaped differently on each side. The side with the round edge will become the inside of the basket. The side with the straight edge will be the outside, or bottom, of the basket.

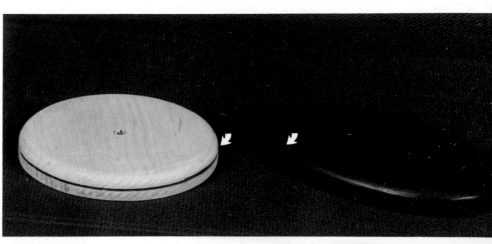

Arrow points to rounded side (inside) of basket base.

2. Sand both sides of the base, and pay special attention to the inside (rounded) side. When the basket is finished it will be difficult to easily sand this side again.

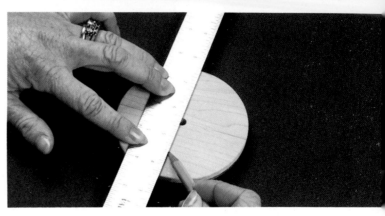

4. Holding the outside of the base facing you, divide the base into quadrants and mark lightly with a pencil. These marks are to aid you in placement of the staves.

3. Finish the inside of the base with the wood treatment you prefer. I usually treat the outside of the base after the basket is made, as a finished base could be marred during the construction process.

5. Bolt the base onto the mold. Have the outside of the base(with the pencil marks) facing you.

Determining the Number of Staves

1. I usually plan on ten six-millimeter cane staves for each diameter inch of mold. As we are using a seven-inch mold, the staves would number seventy. However, a continually woven basket such as a Nantucket Lightship Basket must have an odd number of staves.

2. I probably would use seventy-one cane staves to insure a pleasing, fully staved effect. However, it is easier for a beginner to start a basket with fewer staves. Thus, for this first basket, I would recommend sixty-seven staves.

When you have made a few baskets and feel more comfortable about beginning the basket, you could try to increase the number of staves used. But beware of overstaving! When there are too many staves, the spaces between them are too narrow and it becomes impossible to push the weavers close together in the tight weave that is a hallmark of the Nantucket Lightship Basket.

Preparing the Staves

1. Insert a piece of six-millimeter cane into the slot of the base and bend it up over the side of the mold. Cut the piece one-half inch higher than the top of the mold.

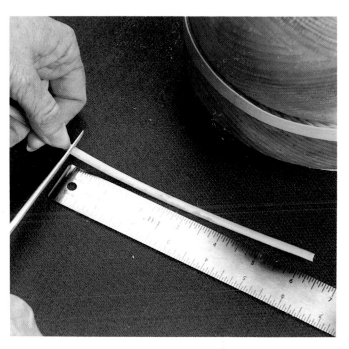

2. Cut sixty-seven pieces of cane this long.

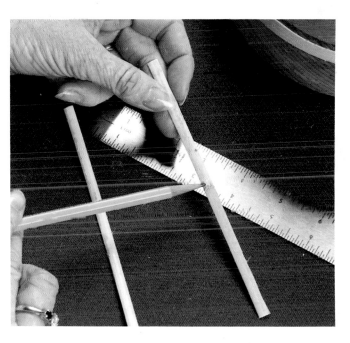

Avoid "knots" or joints in the cane as these detract from the appearance and strength of the basket.

The lengths of cane will differ from one another in color. Some basket makers prefer a monochromatic appearance for both staves and weavers and are quite selective in choosing pieces of similarly colored cane. I prefer a more variegated look with subtle shadings of cane. To achieve this I pull lengths of cane from the bunch at random.

3. In order to fit all sixty-seven staves into the base, one end of each stave must be tapered. The length of the taper is related to the curve of the mold. You must trim the stave to the point where it has passed the curve of the mold. (A more abrupt curve requires less tapering than does a mold with a longer, more gradual curve.)

Arrows mark points to which you need to taper the staves on these two differently curved molds.

Decide on the length of the taper your mold will require.

Pencil denotes place to which stave must be tapered for use on this mold.

106

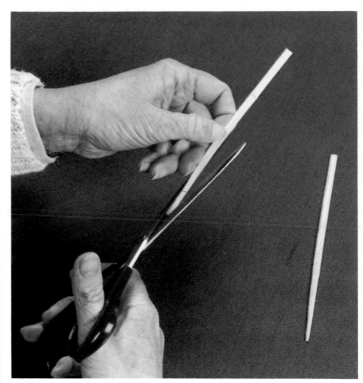

Trim both sides of the bottom of the stave with a knife or scissors.

Inserting the Staves and Weaving First Row

There are two similar methods to begin a basket. I usually weave the first row as I insert the staves (Method 2). However, it will be easier for your first basket to insert the staves without having to grapple with the weaver (Method 1). With this method you will weave the first row after the staves have been inserted and dried.

Method 1

1. Place a heavy elastic band around the top of the mold. This will hold the staves in place while they dry.

2. Soak the staves in water for about two or three minutes. If using oak, soak the staves until they are pliable.

3. Dividing the number of staves by four, we will have seventeen staves in three of the quadrants of the base and sixteen staves in the fourth.

4. Insert the tapered end of a stave, with the shiny side of the cane facing you, into the slot of the base. The stave should fit snugly. However, if it is too thick to fit in the slot, thin it slightly with your knife.

Place the remaining sixteen staves evenly throughout the first quadrant of the basket.

5. Check the spacing between the staves to insure that it is even and that there is enough room between the staves to fit the weaver that eventually will be placed there. If there is not enough space between staves, remove the staves and taper the lower edges more. (There should be approximately one sixteenth of an inch between the staves.)

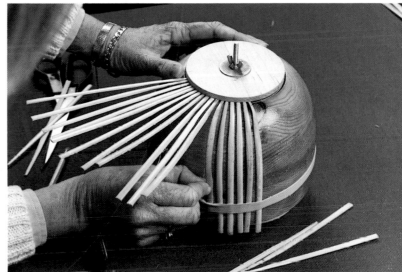

6. When you are pleased with the spacing, secure the ends of the staves under the rubber band and

insert the remaining staves evenly around the base.

Weaving the Body of the Basket

1. Finish weaving row 2 and proceed to row 3. In these first few rows it is important to keep the rows of weaving as close together as possible. The first row should touch the wooden base, the second row should touch the first row, the third row touch the second, and so forth.

I am always pushing the newly woven rows down with my fingernails. However, after one or two baskets, these-my best tools-have worn down and I turn for help to a screwdriver to gently push the weavers close together.

Keeping the weaver slightly damp also will facilitate your control of it.

2. Continue weaving over and under, one stave at a time, while maintaining a tight tension on the weaver. This tension will cause the basket to grip the mold as you weave around the curve of the mold. Holding the staves firmly against the mold also will help the basket conform to the curve.

Note the curved sides. They result from weaving too loosely around the curve and/or too tightly on the body of the basket.

3. As you weave, adjust the staves so that they are straight (perpendicular to the base of the basket). Maintaining an equal distance between staves helps assure alignment.

As you begin to weave around the curve of the mold, turn the mold so that you are holding it on its side. In this way you can see the position of the staves relative to the side of the mold and assure that they are straight. (Staves often tend to tilt in the direction of the weaving.) I am con-

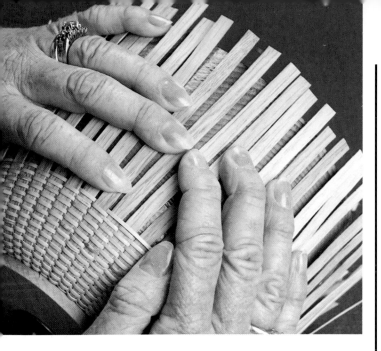

stantly adjusting the position of the staves throughout the weaving of the basket to insure that they are properly aligned.

4. When you weave under a stave, try to move the stave as little as possible.

Pulling the stave away from the mold in order to place the weaver underneath can cause the stave to snap.

5. As mentioned previously it is desirable to have the basket tightly gripping the mold as you weave around the curve. However, it is not necessary for such a tension to be maintained once the curve has been rounded. In fact, if the weaver is too tight and actually holds the mold in a "death grip" as you proceed up the side of the mold, it will be difficult to remove the basket from the mold.

The basket should grip the mold more tightly around the curve than around the sides of the basket. Thus once you have woven around the curve,

release the tension of the weaver and weave three or four staves at a time.

If you have accurately tapered the staves, the rounding of the curve will correspond to the end of the taper.

111

6. To begin a new weaver, you must weave over the old weaver for a short distance. End the old weaver by clipping it off as it goes over the last stave(stave number 4).

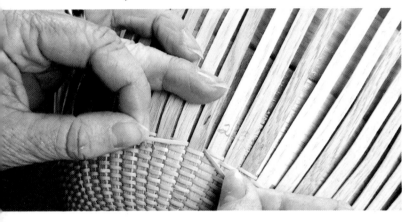

Count back four staves to the left (stave number 1). Slip the new weaver over the old weaver and under stave number 1.

Continue *over* stave number 2, *under* number 3, and *over* number 4.

The new weaver should be hiding the old weaver.

You are ready to continue weaving.

7. Continue to push one row down close to the row below it. A Nantucket Lightship Basket is judged by its close, tight weave. Each row should touch the row above and below it, with no "holes" visible. (Once you have released the horizontal tension of the weaver, it will be easier to push the rows together.) Weave to the top of the mold.

Preparing the Rim

1. To properly construct the rims of the basket, you should use a mold on which to form the rims. Although you can bend wet reed into a circular shape, careful molding of all elements of the basket is part of the precise process of constructing a basket. If a rim mold did not come with the basket mold you received, you can make one fairly easily.

    With a compass, draw a circle the same diameter as the mold on a piece of wood. Next, draw another circle whose diameter is 3/8" smaller.

The outer rim is cut in the same fashion except that in this instance you hold the flat side of the reed against the outer rim.

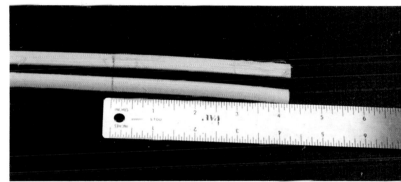

    Cut out the two circles with a band saw. The larger circle will be the "outer" rim, the smaller the "inner rim". (For convenience I usually glue the two circles together.)

2. To determine the length of the inner rim, lay a piece of 3/8" half-round reed with the rounded side against the inner rim. Overlap the end over the remainder of the reed about four inches. Mark the point where the end of the reed touches the body of the reed. Cut the reed at this point.

3. The ends of each rim must be tapered in order to form an attractive "scarf joint." Mark the rounded side of the inner rim four inches from one end. Turn the rim over and mark the flat side four inches from the opposite end. Mark the outer rim in the same way. Each rim should have one pencil mark on the round side and one pencil mark on the flat side.

4. Plane the rounded side of the inner rim from the mark to the end of the rim. You need to take less reed off the rim near the mark and more reed off the rim near the end so that the cut will be on an angle. To do this, place the plane near the end of the reed and make a few passes with the plane.

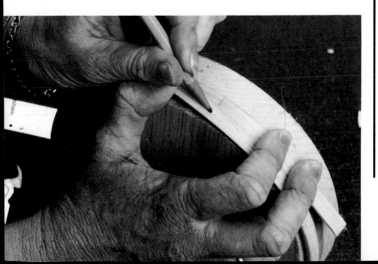

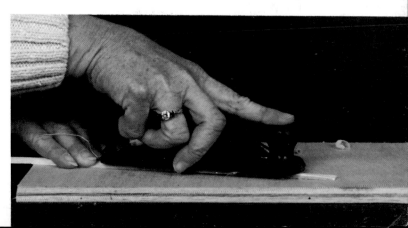

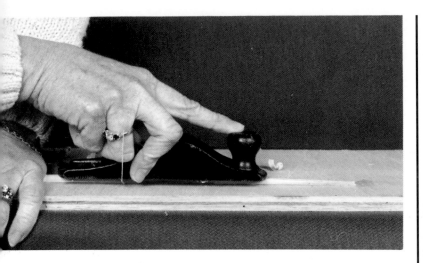

Next, set the plane nearer to the pencil mark and shave from there to the end of the reed.

Finally, place the plane on the pencil mark and shave to the end of the reed. Each cut will thin the reed at the end, but take less material off near the pencil mark. The end can be almost tissue thin.

5. Plane the rounded side of the outer rim in a similar manner.

6. Next, turn the rims over and plane where marked on the flat sides of each rim, again planing from the mark to the end. Leave more reed near the mark and take off more reed near the end of the rim. You have now "scarfed" the rims.

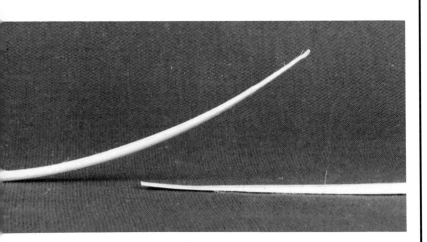

The flat side has been planed on the rim at left whereas the right rim has been planed on its rounded side.

You also may scarf the rims by holding them against a power sander. This speedier method requires a steady hand so that not too much reed will be sanded away.

Molding the Rims

1. Soak the rims in warm water for ten or fifteen minutes or until they are pliable.

2. Take the inner rim, place it with its rounded side against the inner rim mold, overlap the ends, and nail it to the mold with a brass escutcheon pin.

Repeat the process with the outer rim, making sure to lay the flat side against the outer rim mold.

3. Let the rim dry for a few days.

Placing the Rims on the Basket

The following Steps 1 through 7 assume that you have woven the basket to the top of the mold. If you prefer a finished basket whose height is shorter than the mold, use Method 2 to place the rims.

Method 1

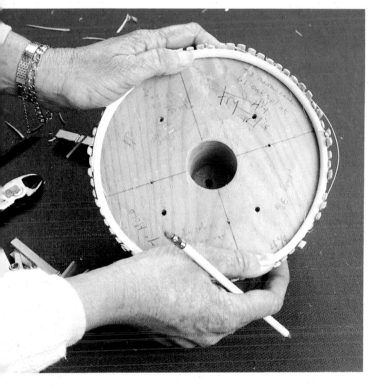

1. Carefully take the inner rim off the rim mold. Place it inside the basket. (The basket remains on the basket mold.)

2. Spread the rim out gently so that its flat side is touching the staves but not pushing on them. Mark a point where one edge of the rim touches the other.

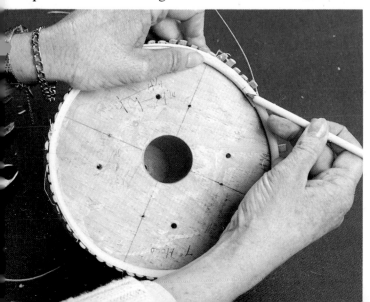

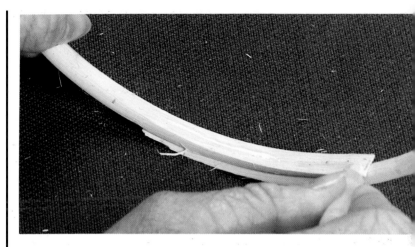

Remove the rim from the basket and spread glue along the planed section of the rim.

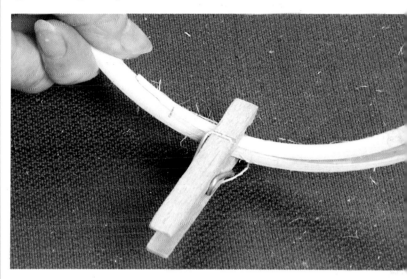

I use fast-drying cyanoacrylate glue. The benefit-the speed in which it sets-is obvious. However, if you have not marked the rim carefully, it can be extremely difficult if not impossible to separate the rims again. Press the two ends together to match the two pencil marks. Use clamps or snap clothespins to hold the joint while the glue dries.

3. When the glue has dried (which takes five minutes maximum), take the rim and place it back inside the basket. Remove the outer rim from its mold and clamp it around the outside of the basket as tightly as you can.

115

Again make a pencil mark at a point where the edges of the rim are touching each other. Remove the rim from the basket.

The outer rim should fit snugly on the basket when completed. To achieve this I glue this rim ever so slightly tighter than my pencil marks.

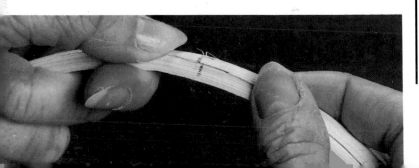

In a choice between an outer rim that is too tight or one that is too loose, I would choose one that is too tight. It is possible to sand down the inside of a tight outer rim. However, it is impossible to alter a rim that is too loose without taking the joint apart and starting over.

4. Glue and clamp the outer rim.

5. When the glue on the outer rim has dried, try placing both rims on the basket to check their fit. If satisfactory, remove the outer rim and cut off the tops of the staves level with the top of the inner rim.

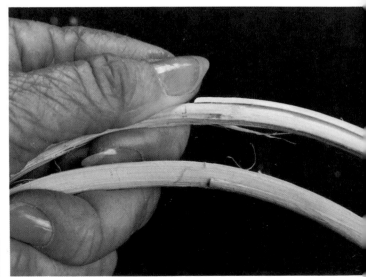

6. The joints on each rim undoubtedly will be visible at best and unattractive at worst.

To enhance their appearance, whittle and sand the edges of the joint where one piece of reed meets the other.

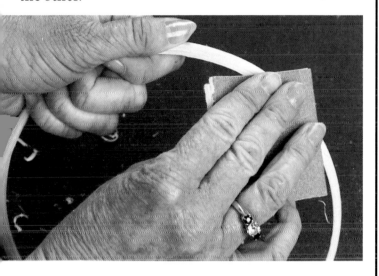

Careful finishing of these joints should leave them all but invisible.

More practice will produce more perfect scarf joints.

7. Remove the basket from the mold. Although the mold will give you some resistance when you first try to pull off the basket, removing the basket should not be too difficult a task. If it is a herculean undertaking, there is a good chance that either you wove too tightly or your staves were not perfectly straight.

Method 2

Use this method when you prefer to stop weaving your basket before you reach the top of the mold.

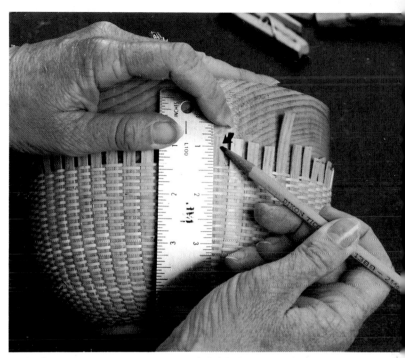

1. On one stave measure 3/8" higher than the top row of weaving and mark that stave.

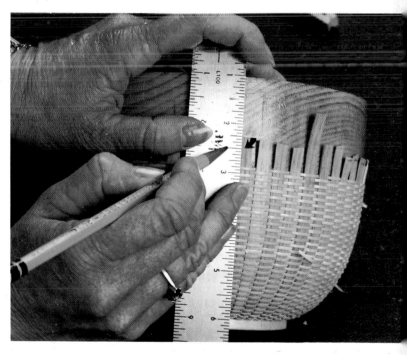

2. Measure from the top of the mold to the pencil mark on the stave. On the basket illustrated, this measurement was 1 1/2".

117

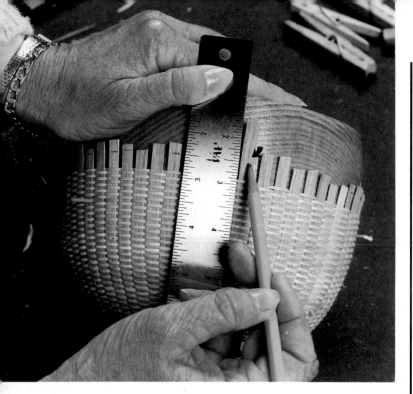

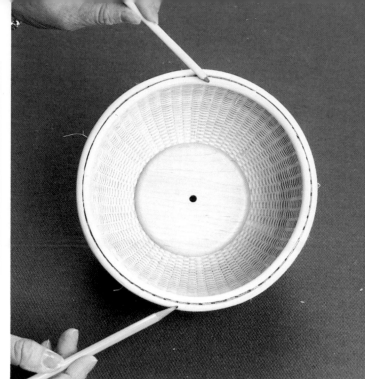

3. Finally mark all staves 1 1/2" down from the top of the mold.

4. Remove the basket from the mold. Cut the staves at the pencil marks.

5. Place the inner rim inside the basket. Proceed as in Steps 1 through 6 of Method 1.

Nailing the Rims

1. Before placing the rims on the basket, look inside the basket at the wooden base. Turn the basket so that the grain of the wood of the base is running from left to right.

If you think of the grain as running east to west, place the inner rim in the basket with its joint at the southern position. Then place the outer rim on the basket with its joint at the northern position. Joints are placed opposite each other in this way both for aesthetics and for strength.

Basket makers have differing attitudes toward the brass escutcheon pins used for nailing the rims. Some do not like to see the pins at all. They countersink them and fill the holes with wood filler. Others, such as myself, enjoy the look of the pins. I believe it to be one of the distinctive features of a Nantucket Lightship Basket.

You also will find differences in the number of pins placed in the rim. Some basket makers put one pin through each stave, some through every other stave, and some through every third stave. Try to visualize the appearance that you will find attractive and place the pins accordingly. Mark each stave in which you wish to put a pin with a light pencil dot on the rim over that stave.

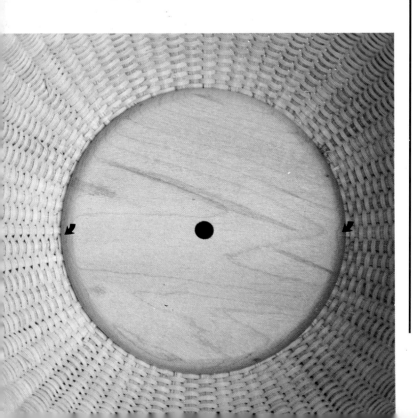

2. While holding the basket in front of you, turn it slowly and take a critical look at the rim to see if it appears to be level all the way around. If it does not, move the rims up or down where necessary.

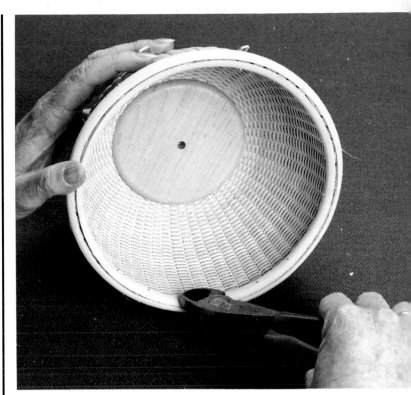

3. At each pencil dot, drill through the rims and stave. You will need a hobby drill that can take bits small enough to match the size of the escutcheon pins you use. I use number 20 escutcheon pins and a #65 guage drill bit.

4. Insert five escutcheon pins spaced evenly around the rim. These will keep the rim from shifting while you place the remaining pins in their respective holes.

5. When all pins are in, snip off the pointed end of any pin that shows on the inside of the basket.

6. Hold the basket on its side and rest the head of an escutcheon pin on a hard surface such as metal. Bend over the cut end of this pin by gently striking it with a ballpeen hammer.

The head of the pin should remain resting against the hard surface while you hammer. Repeat this technique with the remaining pins and try to bend all the ends in the same direction so that the inside of the inner rim looks attractive.

7. Sand the rim to remove any marks left by the hammer.

Lashing the Rim

1. Use the carriage fine cane to lash the rim. In addition, you will need a piece of "common" cane as a filler piece. This filler piece lies on top of the rim of the basket and hides the stave ends that you see between the rims.

2. Insert a piece of carriage fine lasher into one of the spaces between two staves.

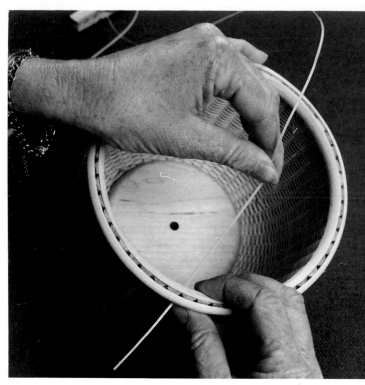

Pull the lasher to the inside until about two inches of lasher remain sticking out the front of the basket.

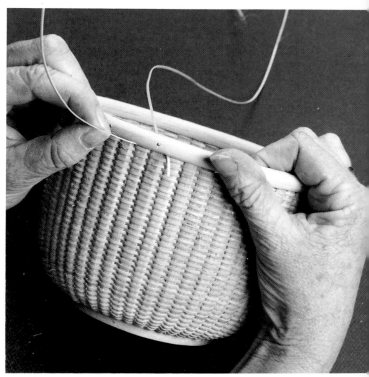

3. Bring the long end of the lasher that remains inside the basket out to the front of the basket and insert it through the first space to the left. Pull the lasher through the space to the inside once more. Do not completely tighten the loop.

4. Repeat this procedure four more times. You now should have four loops around the rim. Take the "tail" of the lasher that is sticking out the front of the basket and lay it to the left, under the rim and under the loops of the lasher.

7. You want to keep tight tension on the lasher to prevent the loops from sliding around. So that I do not lose whatever tension I achieved, I always put a clothespin on the last loop I have lashed.

8. Continue lashing the basket. Keep the filler piece positioned securely to hide the split between the rims.

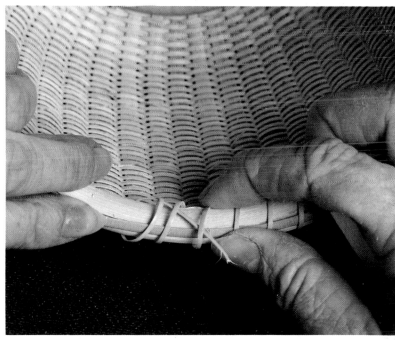

5. Before tightening the loops completely, lay the filler piece of common cane on top of the rim of the basket, under the loops. Leave about one inch of filler piece laying beyond the right of the first loop.

6. Now tighten the loops of the lasher one at a time and catch the filler piece on top and the tail of the lasher under the rim.

9. If the lasher breaks or ends naturally, you must secure the end and begin a new piece. To secure the end, first loosen the last three or four loops you have formed. Next, tuck the end of the lasher along the rim on the inside of the basket and catch it under the last three or four loops.

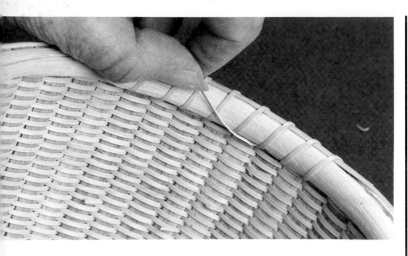

Tighten the loops.

10. Begin the new piece of lasher as you began the old. The space in which you will insert the new lasher is the same space in which the old lasher ended. That is, two pieces of cane will be sharing the same space.

If you incorrectly insert the lasher through the first empty space to the left, you will have a gap in your loops.

11. As you near the end of the lashing, do not tighten the last three or four loops.

12. Lay one end of the filler piece over the other and cut through both pieces at a point where a loop of lashing will be able to hide the joint.

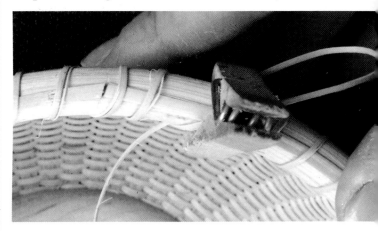

The ends of the filler now will butt up against each other. `

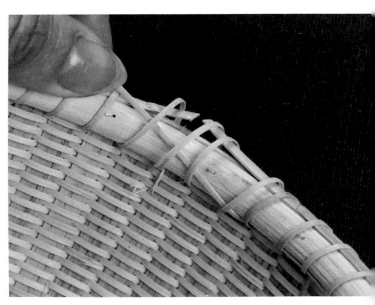

Place the tail of the lasher inside the rim and under the last three or four loops.

Tighten the loops. If necessary, glue the filler ends at the joint to keep them in place.

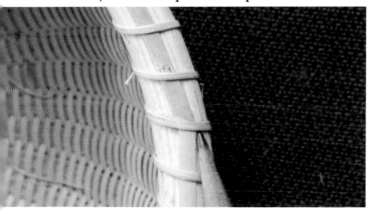

Be sure to cover the joint of the filler piece with one of the loops of the lasher.

The Handle

1. Sand and treat your handle with the finish you prefer.

You will need a drill bit whose size matches the pin or rivet that you will be using to secure the handle.

2. Drill a hole in each end of the handle where it will be mounted on the basket rim.

3. Hold the basket with the grain of the wooden base again running right to left. The handle also will run right to left, along with the grain. Choose two locations on the rim, points directly over a stave, at which to mount the handle.

As you look down on the positioned handle and basket, the handle should bisect the basket. If it is not centered properly, adjust the handle.

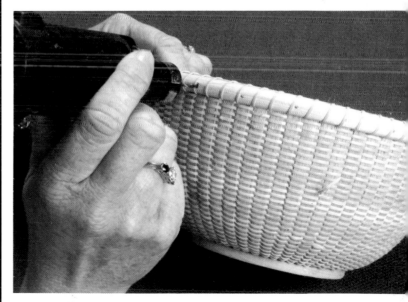

4. Drill through the outer rim, stave, and inner rim at the two points you have selected.

5. Attach the handle with the fastener of your choice. I use a number 14 brass escutcheon pin that I fasten by hammering its end over a copper burr (washer) of the same size.

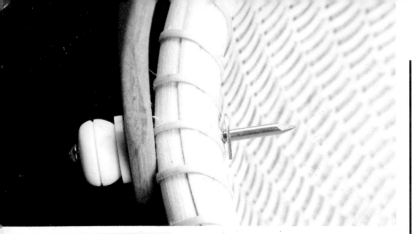

6. If you choose this method, insert the pin through the ivory fitting (optional), the handle, and the basket rim, and the burr.

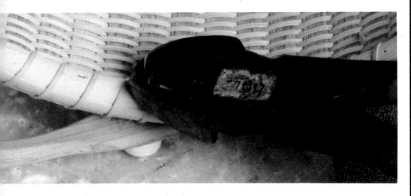

7. Using wire snips, clip the pointed end of the pin almost level with the copper burr.

8. Place the head of the pin against a hard surface such as metal and mash the pin end down over the burr with a ballpeen hammer.

You also may solder this connection for added strength.

Finishing

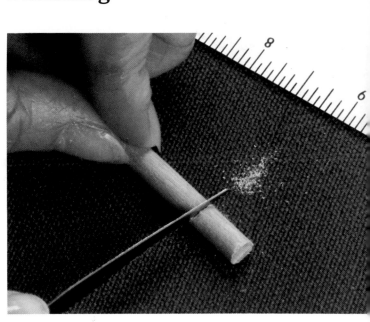

1. You will fill the hole in the bottom of the base with a short length of dowel. The hole drilled through my bases is 1/4", thus I use 1/4" dowel. Cut the piece of dowel the same length as the thickness of your base. As my bases are 1/2" thick, I cut the dowel 1/2" long.

You may need to trim the dowel end slightly to start it in the hole.

Hammer the dowel into the hole.

Sand off any excess dowel that protrudes from the base.

2. Trim any pieces of cane on the basket as necessary.

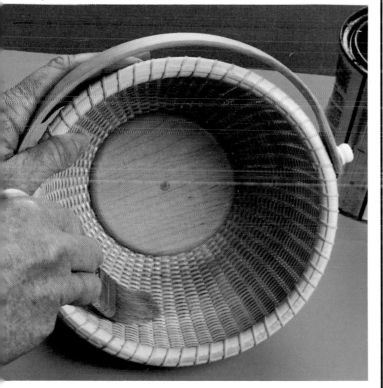

3. Finish the basket with a preservative. You can use shellac or polyurethane. Shellac, which dries faster, is the finish you will find on old baskets. It reacts with ultraviolet light and a basket will darken or age more quickly with shellac. Polyurethaned baskets also will age, however. I usually brush one coat of finish on the inside of the basket and two on the outside.

4. After all of this effort, it is fun to sign your basket. You may use an engraving bit in your drill, a wood-burning tool, or even a ball-point pen.

5. Sand and finish the outside, or bottom, of the wooden base.

Hundreds of my students have not only created lovely round Nantucket Lightship Baskets following the directions given in this book, but have gone on to make other shapes and sizes. Their faces attest to the joy and sense of accomplishment derived from creating such wonderful treasures.

Bibliography

Adamson, Hans. *Keepers of the Lights*. New York: Greenburg, 1955.

Aude, Karen. "Basketry, The Nantucket Island Craft." *Cape Cod Life*, Spring 1983, pp. 46-51.

The Boston Globe. July 8, 1985, p. 21.

Carpenter, Charles H., Jr. "A Cabinetmaker's Baskets in the Nantucket Tradition." *Fine Woodworking*, November/December 1985, pp. 84-87.

Carpenter, Charles H., Jr., and Mary Grace. *The Decorative Arts and Crafts of Nantucket*. New York: Dodd, Mead and Company, 1987.

Crèvecoeur, J. Hector St. John. *Letters from an American Farmer*. New York: Fox, Duffield and Company, 1904.

Crosby, Everett U. *Signs and Silver of Old Time Nantucket*. Nantucket, Mass.: Inquirer and Mirror Press, 1940.

Eaton, Allen H. *Handicrafts of New England*. New York: Bonanza Books, 1949.

Farnham, Joseph E.C. *Brief Historical Data and Memories of My Boyhood Days in Nantucket*. Providence, Rhode Island: Snow and Farnham Company, 1923.

Hemphill, Mary Ann. "The Nantucket Lightship Basket." *Cape Cod Compass*, Holiday 1989, pp. 56-66.

"José Reyes." *The Inquirer and Mirror*, December 31, 1980.

McGinley, Art. "A Personal Chat with A Nantucket Basket Maker." *The Inquirer and Mirror*, September 29, 1945.

McMullen, Ann. *Artifacts*. American Indian Archaeological Institute, Fall 1982.

"A Nantucket Artist Plies His Basket Trade." *The New Bedford Standard Times*, October 13, 1946.

"Nantucket Lightship Baskets." *Colonial Homes*, February 1988, pp. 80-82.

Pappas-Graber, Elaine. "The Art of Buying Lightship Baskets." *Cape Cod Life*, October/November 1987, pp. 94-97.

Putnam, George R. *Lighthouses and Lightships of the U.S.* Boston: Houghton Mifflin, 1917.

Seeler, Katherine and Edgar. *Nantucket Lightship Baskets*. Nantucket, Mass.: The Deermouse Press, 1972.

Slade, Marilyn Myers. "Nantucket Lightship Baskets." *Americana*, July/August 1978, pp. 64-68.

Stackpole, Edouard A. *Life-Saving Nantucket*. Nantucket, Mass: Stern-Majestic Press, Inc., 1972.

Starbuck, Mary Eliza. *My House and I*. Boston: Houghton Mifflin, 1929.

Talbot, F.A. *Lightships and Lighthouses*. Philadelphia: J. B. Lippincott, 1913.

Thompson, Frederic L. *The Lightships of Cape Cod*. Portland, Maine: Congress Square Press, 1983.

Turner, Harry B. "The Nantucket South Shoals Station and the Vessels That Have Guarded It From 1854-1931." *The Inquirer and Mirror*, May 16, 1931.

Whitten, Paul F. *The Friendship Baskets and Their Maker*, José Formoso Reyes.

Wilkinson, Carolyn. "How to Make a Nantucket Lightship Basket." *Woman's Day*, July 1949.

Williams, Winston F. "Floating Lighthouses Warned Sailors for 131 Years." *Cape Cod Life*, October/November 1989, pp. 74-79.

Willoughby, Malcolm F. *Lighthouses of New England*. Boston: T.O. Metcalf Co., 1929.